52 Holiday Wood Projects

John A. Nelson

STERLING PUBLISHING CO., INC.
NEW YORK

Acknowledgments

I especially wish to thank my wife, Joyce, for helping with the writing, typing, and painting of many of these projects. She has a special "touch" that I don't have which adds a nice effect to many of these projects. I thank my youngest daughter, Jennifer, for spending her winter break from college helping finish up the last of the projects. Being a graphic arts major, she helped add a lot to this book.

Thanks to John Woodside, editorial director, Rodman Neumann, editor, and others of the fine staff at STERLING PUBLISHING COMPANY who helped transform my rough manuscript and artwork into this fun-filled book. Last but not least, thanks to Deborah Porter Hayes, who took all of the photographs. Her talents are always appreciated.

Surely without the help of all these people this book would never have been written or produced.

Library of Congress Cataloging-in-Publication Data

Nelson, John A., 1935–
    52 holiday wood projects / John A. Nelson.
       p. cm.
    Includes index.
    ISBN 0-8069-0652-9
    1. Woodwork—Patterns. 2. Holiday decorations. I. Title.
    II. Title: Fifty-two holiday wood projects.
    TT180.N46 1995
    745.594'1—dc20   94-42100
                                          CIP

Edited by Rodman Neumann

1 3 5 7 9 10 8 6 4 2

Published by Sterling Publishing Company, Inc.
387 Park Avenue South, New York, N.Y. 10016
© 1995 by John A. Nelson
Distributed in Canada by Sterling Publishing
% Canadian Manda Group, One Atlantic Avenue, Suite 105
Toronto, Ontario, Canada M6K 3E7
Distributed in Great Britain and Europe by Cassell PLC
Villiers House, 125 Strand, London WC2R 0BB, England
Distributed in Australia by Capricorn Link (Australia) Pty Ltd.
P.O. Box 6651, Baulkham Hills, Business Centre, NSW 2153, Australia
Manufactured in the United States of America
All rights reserved

Sterling ISBN 0-8069-0652-9

Contents

Color section follows page 64

INTRODUCTION

This book contains 52 holiday and special occasion projects. There are about 100 full-size patterns. Each is designed to be made over a weekend—all 52 of them. A project for each weekend for a *full* year. Projects range from very simple, one-piece projects to intermediate woodworking level—something for everyone.

I hope these projects will add a personal festive flavor to your home during various holidays throughout the year. There are projects for New Year's Eve, Valentine's Day, St. Patrick's Day, Easter, Fourth of July, Halloween, Thanksgiving, winter holidays, a welcome sign, and three complete alphabets for your use to make up projects for other special occasions or holidays.

Since most projects are rather simple in scope, individual instructions are not given. Anything special is noted on the actual full-size drawing. Almost all of the projects in this book are drawn *full size* for your convenience. However, do not limit yourself to these sizes; feel free to enlarge, reduce, or modify each for *your* individual, particular needs. Be creative—with a little thought you can add your own ideas and finishing touches to make each project a little different and truly "*yours.*"

In finishing and painting your project, do whatever you think would make it look just right. In many cases, *suggested* colors are noted, but do not feel you have to use them. Don't be afraid to experiment with your projects. Add real ribbons, bells, hats, or whatever is to your liking. Have fun.

Copying, Enlarging/Reducing Patterns

The best way to reproduce the patterns in this book (or to enlarge or reduce) is to use an electrostatic copy machine. These machines are found in most offices or libraries. I would suggest you make *two* copies: one for making and cutting out, one for painting details and finishing.

If you want to make a very large pattern, visit a local "quick" printer—almost every town has one. Ask for a P.M.T. (photomechanical transfer) copy. These can be made up to 24 inches by 36 inches or larger. Ask for an extra copy. They are well worth the cost.

Materials

Since these projects require so little material, use the best material you can find. Use high-grade, straight-grain, knot-free wood. When using plywood, try to find marine or aircraft multi-ply, high-quality plywood. Better material will make the *project* go faster and easier—it will end up being a better-finished project.

Preparing the Wood Surfaces

In doing small projects such as those in this book, I like to finish the surfaces *before* I cut the pieces out. Sand and prime the wood on both sides. Apply a base top coat over the primer, and lightly sand all over.

The smoother the surface finish, the more "professional" your project will look. (It is relatively easy to get a nice smooth finish *before* cutting the project out.)

Attaching the Pattern to the Wood

Attach the full-size pattern to the wood by using rubber cement or a spray-mount-type adhesive. Apply the adhesive to the *back* side of the paper pattern. Let it dry thoroughly, and then stick it to the wood. Take care to apply the pattern with any long, thin areas *parallel* or in line with the grain of the wood. The copy will provide you with black lines on a clear, white background. This is great for cutting out small shapes. With a little practice it is fairly simple to split the black line of the pattern with a saw blade. If you stray from the line slightly, don't worry—when you remove the pattern no one will know.

Apply a *blank* piece of paper to the back surface of the wood, also. (Make a sandwich of the paper and wood.) This will eliminate any tears of the wood as you saw the pieces out. It will also provide a nice smooth surface so the wood will slide more easily over the table.

Simply peel the pattern and blank piece of paper from the wood after cutting out. Remove *all* rubber cement or other adhesive residue by simply rubbing it off with your fingers. Be sure to do this before applying any paint.

Finishing Your Project

Use high-quality paint for these projects. I recommend water-base paint since it dries quickly, cleans up easily with water, and provides a high-quality finish. To allow the paint to flow easily, add a little water to the paint to slightly thin it out.

Adding Special Accessories

Visit a *craft shop*—they have lots of scaled-down items such as hats, bows, bells, pipes, etc., to add to the projects. These little touches can add a lot to the project. Use your imagination to make each project *yours*.

Important

If your project will be used by a small child, be sure to use a *nontoxic* paint, and do *not* use any small pieces of wood that a child could swallow. You can use the toilet-roll-tube test—if a piece fits through a cardboard toilet-roll tube, then it is too small and not safe.

THE 52 HOLIDAY WOOD PROJECTS

NEW YEAR'S

1♦Baby with Year

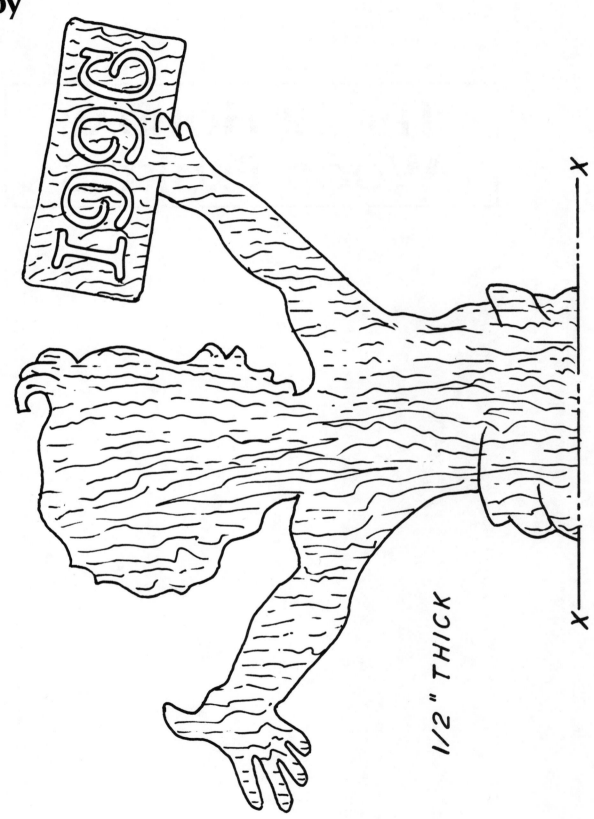

1/2" THICK

1234567890

NUMBERS FOR YEAR →

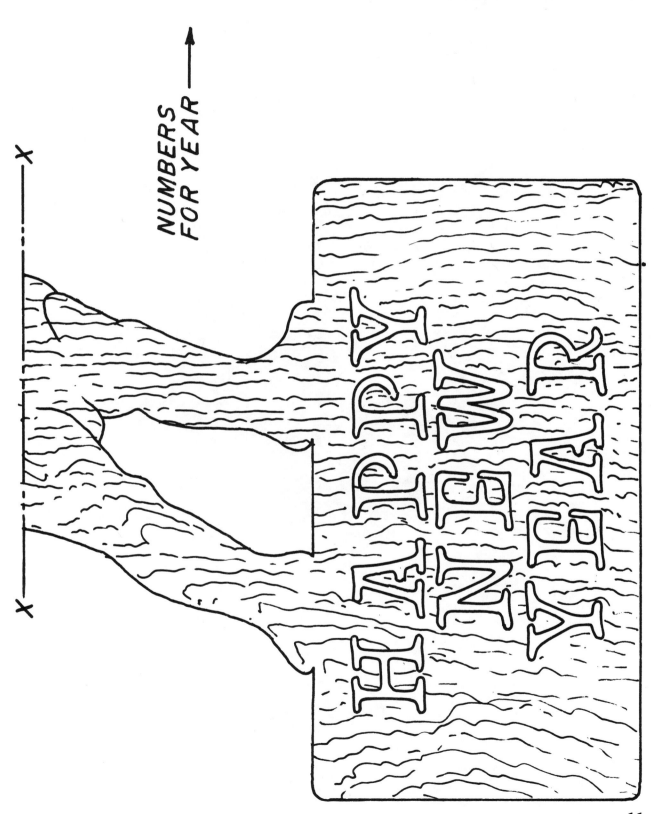

HAPPY NEW YEAR

X — — — X

VALENTINE'S DAY

2♦Love Birds

ASSEMBLY

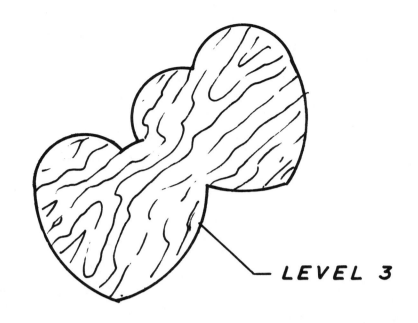

LEVEL 3

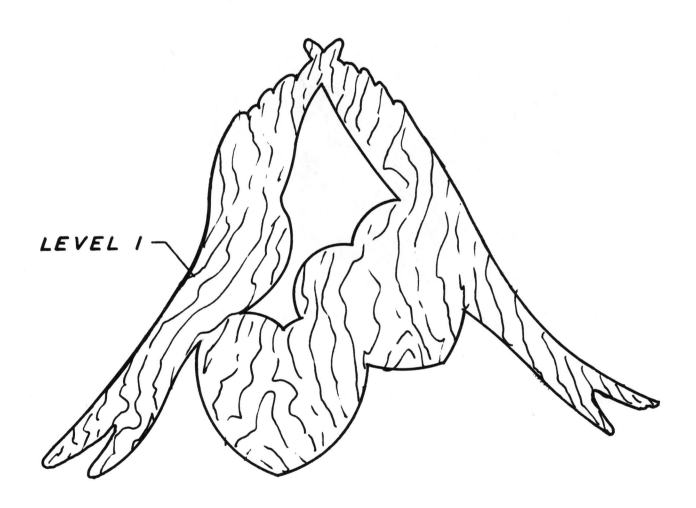

LEVEL 1

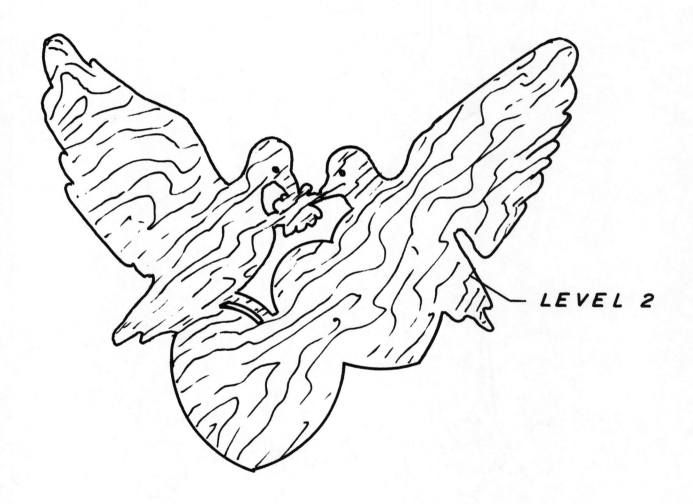

LEVEL 2

3♦Ring of Hearts and Bears

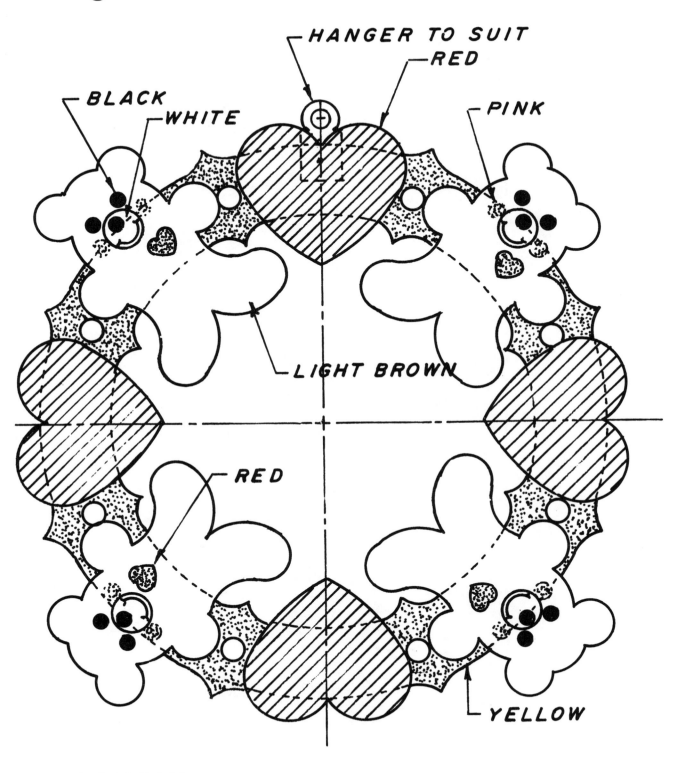

ASSEMBLY
NOT FULLSIZE

GLUE HEARTS AND
BEARS TO BASE AS
SHOWN.

1/4" THICK

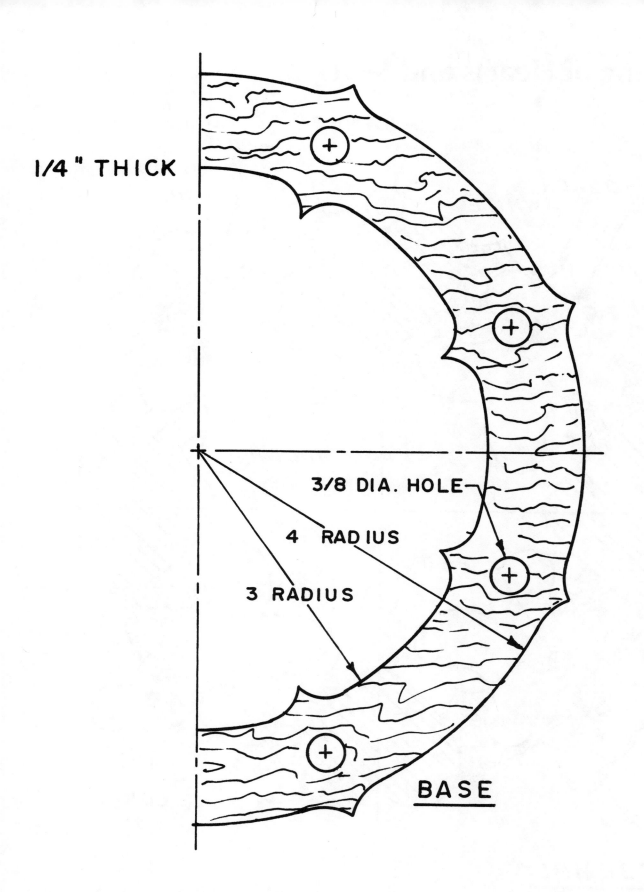

3/8 DIA. HOLE

4 RADIUS

3 RADIUS

BASE

HALF PATTERN

HEART
1/4 " THICK

1/8" THICK

NOSE

1/4" THICK

BEAR

4 ♦ Hanging Bird with a Heart

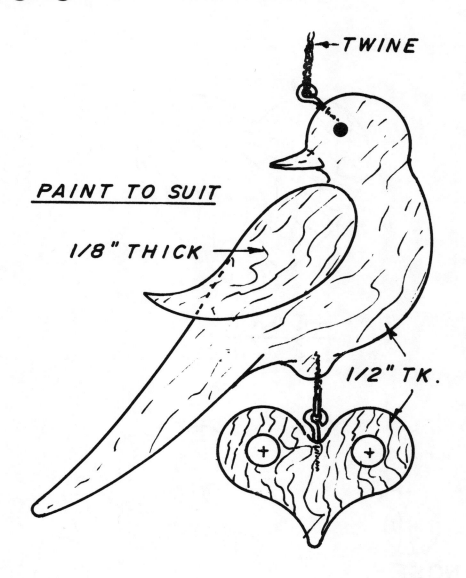

TWINE

PAINT TO SUIT

1/8" THICK

1/2" TK.

OTHER USES FOR HEARTS

STRING

HOLE DIA. TO SUIT

SEE ALPHABET BELOW

PATTERN

A B C D E F
G H I J K L M N O
P Q R S T U V W
X Y Z · 1 2 3 4
5 6 7 8 9 0

PAINT WITH BRIGHT COLORS

5♦Angel on a Shelf with Hearts

5/8" THICK

1/8" THICK

TWINE

3/8" THICK

1/2" THICK

5/8" THICK

LOVE

1/8" DIA. X 6 1/4" LONG

ASSEMBLY
(FRONT VIEW)

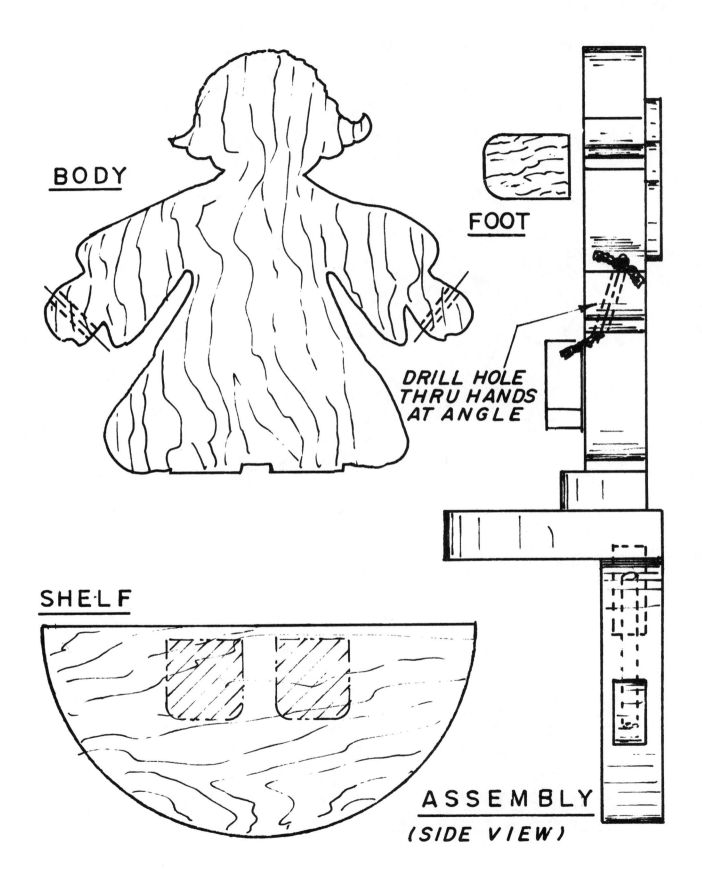

BODY

FOOT

DRILL HOLE
THRU HANDS
AT ANGLE

SHELF

ASSEMBLY
(SIDE VIEW)

6♦Wall Box with Hearts

EXPLODED VIEW

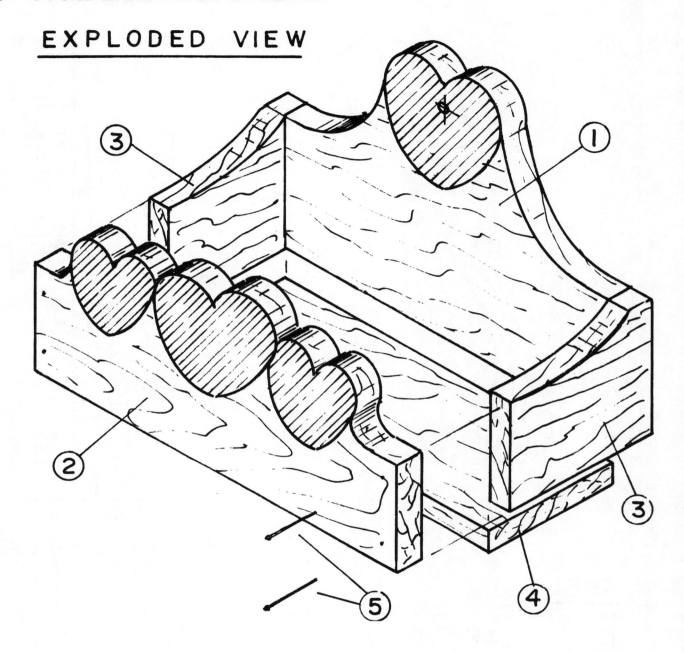

NO.	NAME	SIZE	REQ'D.
1	BACK	1/2 X 6 – 8 LONG	1
2	FRONT	1/2 X 4 – 9 LONG	1
3	END	1/2 X 3 – 3 1/2 LONG	2
4	BOTTOM	1/2 X 3 – 8 LONG	1
5	NAIL – FINISH	6 b	12

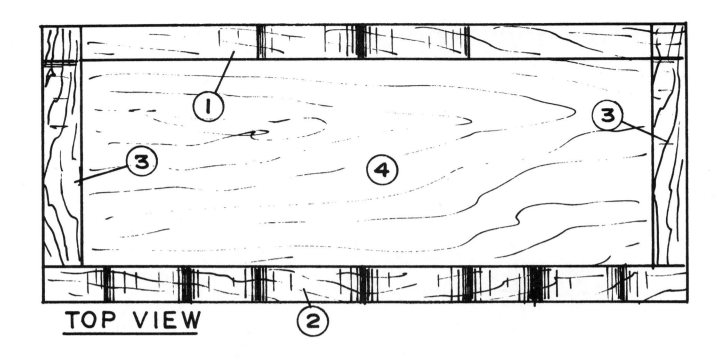

TOP VIEW

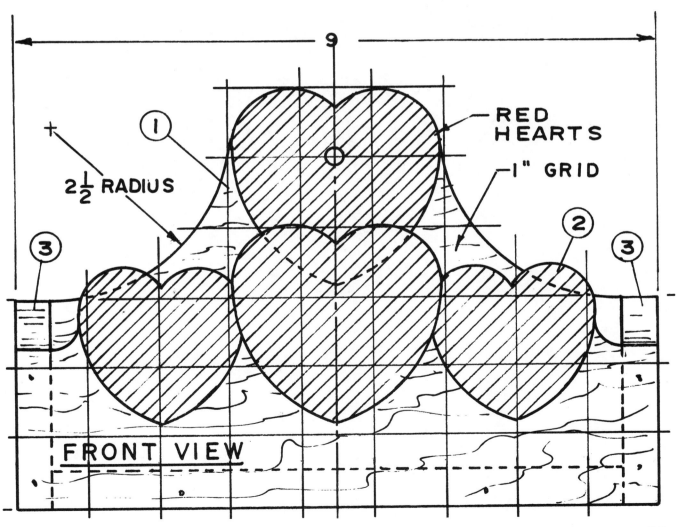

9

① RED HEARTS

$2\frac{1}{2}$ RADIUS

②

③ ③

1" GRID

FRONT VIEW

23

7♦ "I Love You" Signs

8♦Welcome Sign

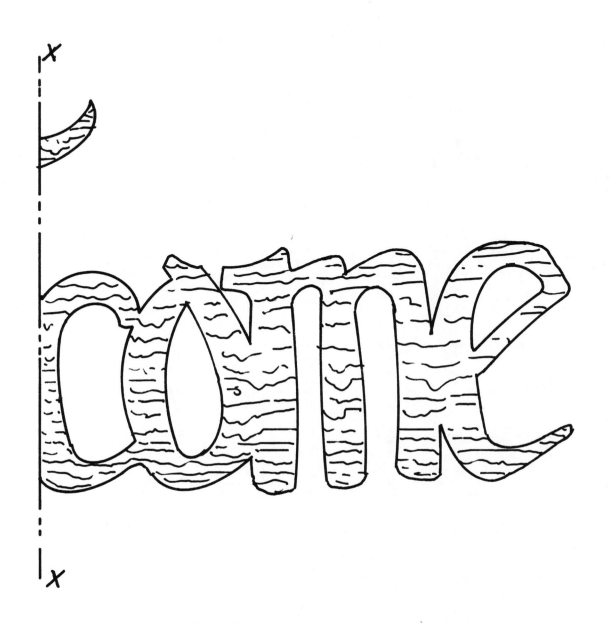

9♦Cupid Silhouette

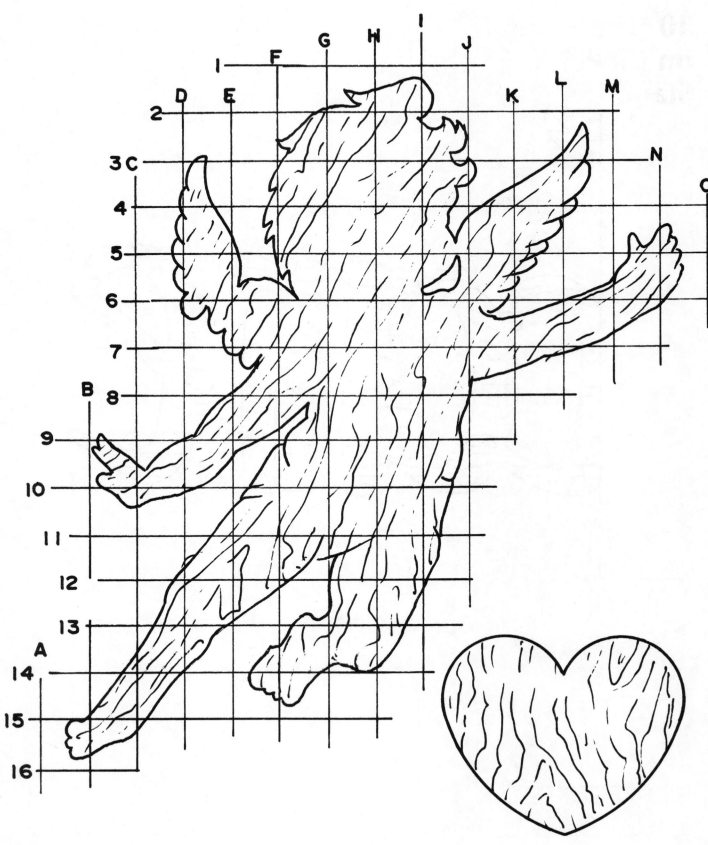

ST. PATRICK'S DAY

10♦Leprechaun on Clover Stand

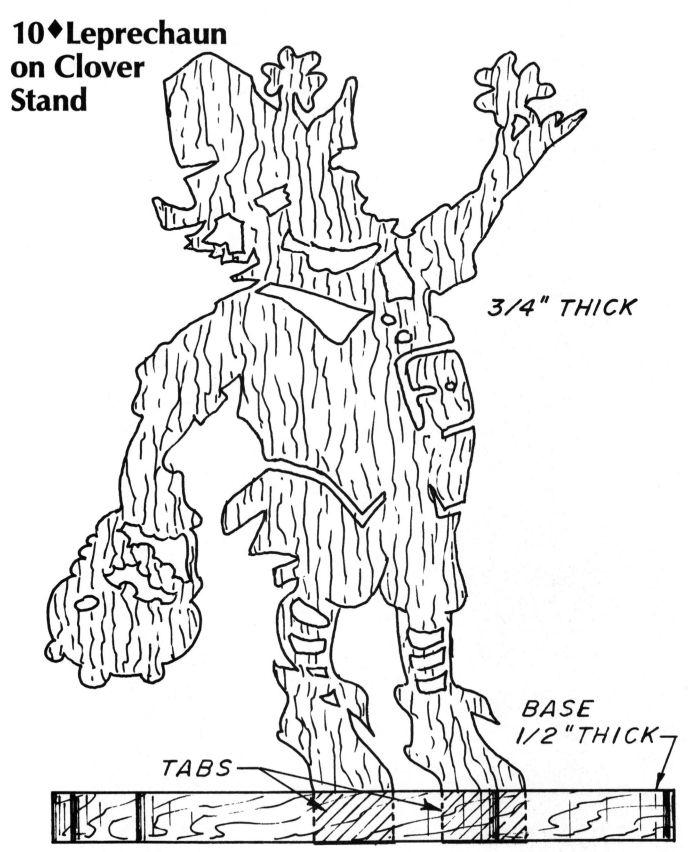

3/4" THICK

BASE 1/2" THICK

TABS

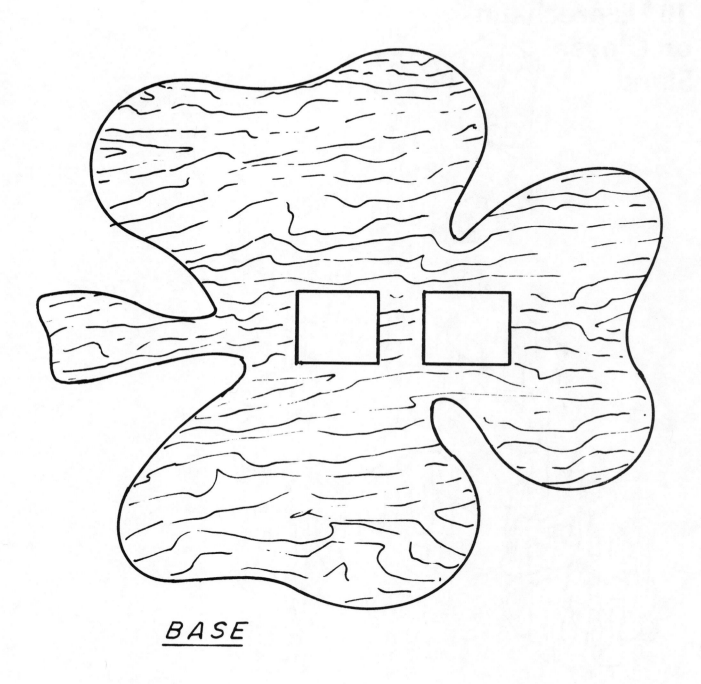

BASE

EASTER

11♦Easter Bunny

(NOT FULLSIZE)

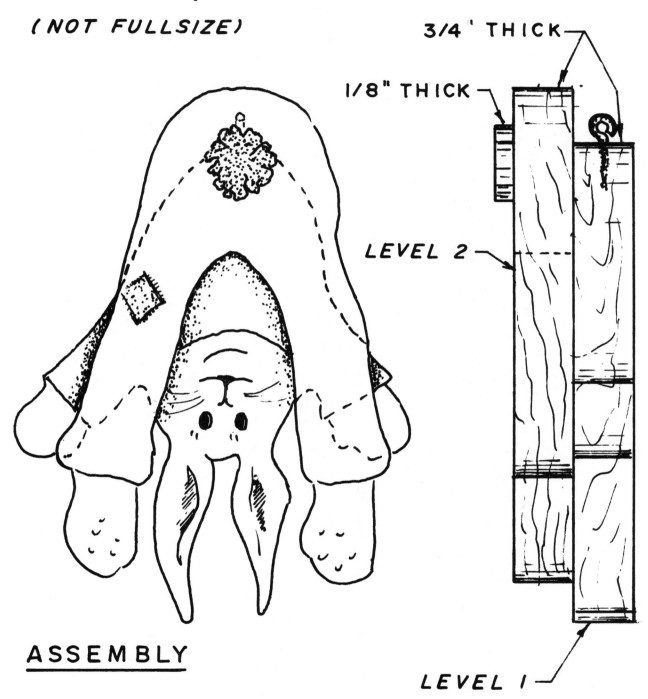

3/4' THICK

1/8" THICK

LEVEL 2

LEVEL 1

ASSEMBLY

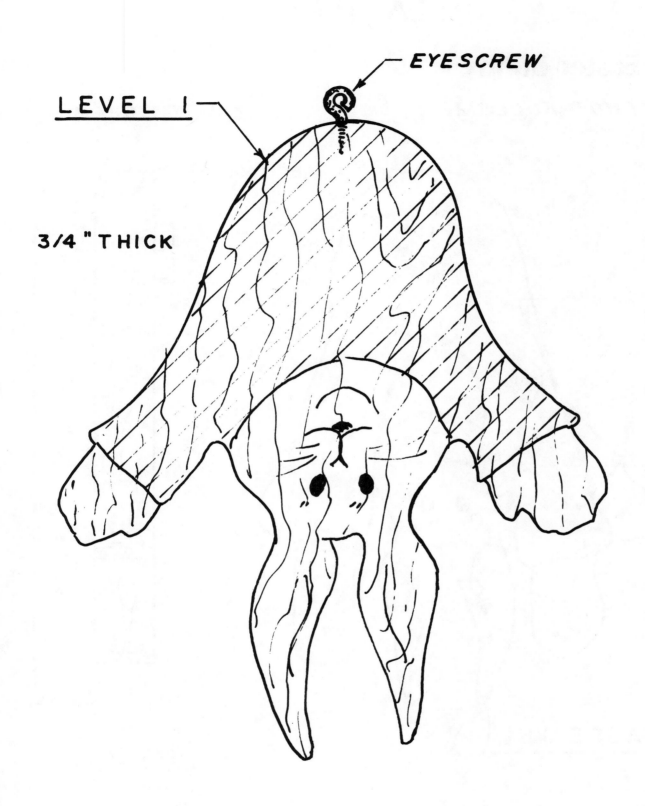

EYESCREW

LEVEL 1

3/4 " THICK

FULLSIZE

32

TAIL

1/8" THICK

3/4 " THICK

LEVEL 2

FULLSIZE

12♦Swan Easter Basket

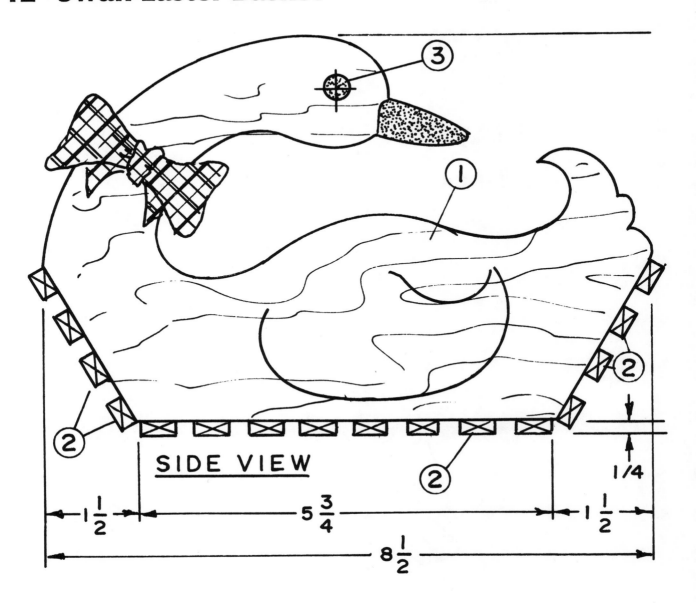

SIDE VIEW

$1\frac{1}{2}$ $5\frac{3}{4}$ $1\frac{1}{2}$

$8\frac{1}{2}$

1/4

NOT FULLSIZE

NOTE: THE ABOVE CAN BE USED FOR A FULLSIZE
PATTERN (SMALL BASKET)

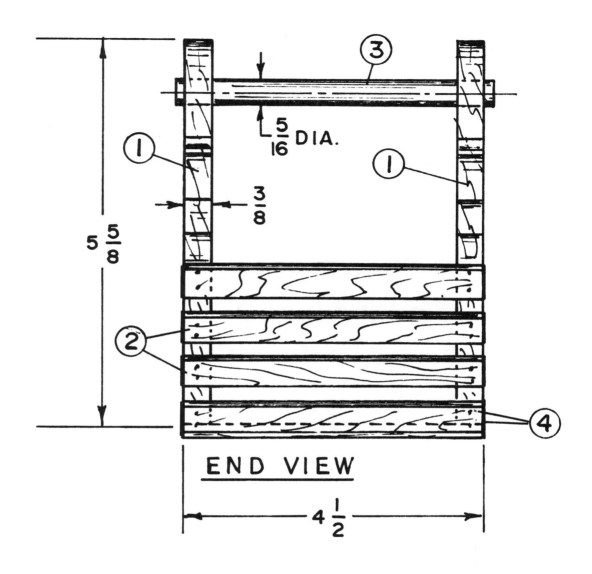

 END VIEW

NO.	NAME	SIZE	REQ'D.
1	SIDE	3/8 X 5 5/8 - 8 1/2	2
2	END / BOTTOM	1/4 X 1/2 - 4 1/2	16
3	HANDLE	5/16 DIA. - 4 3/4	1
4	BRAD	3/4 LONG	64

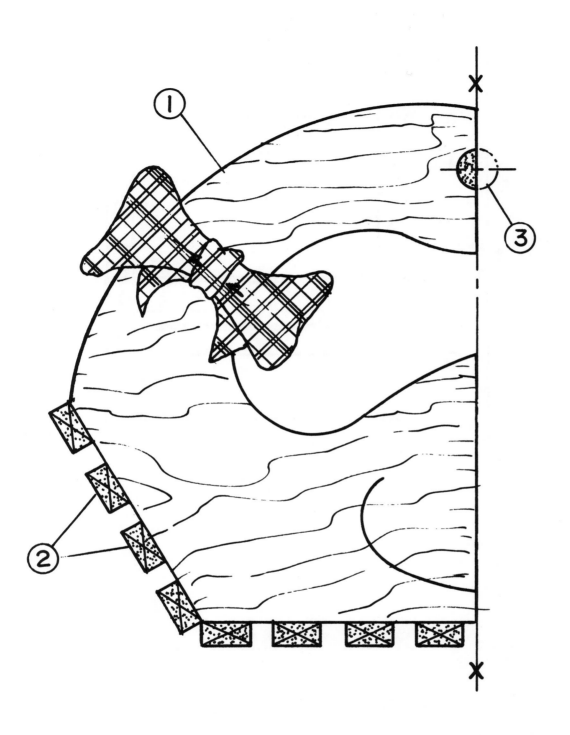

FULLSIZE PATTERN

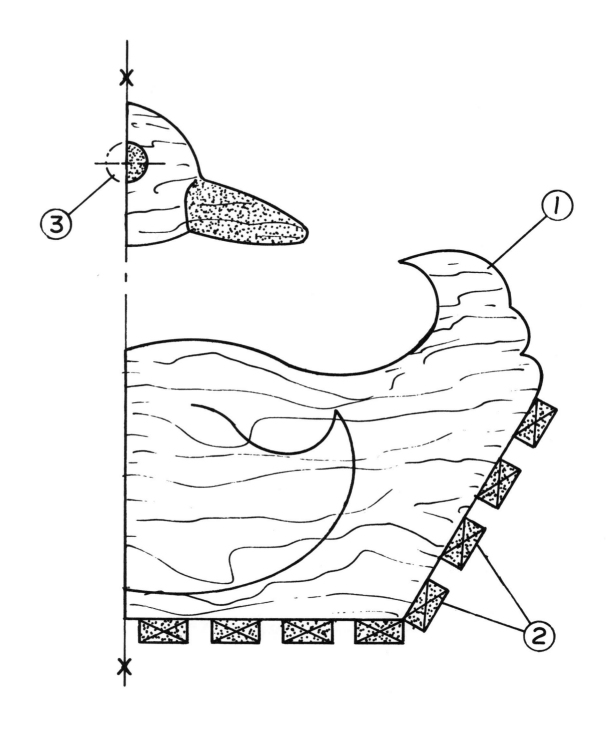

13 ♦ Rabbit Plant Holder

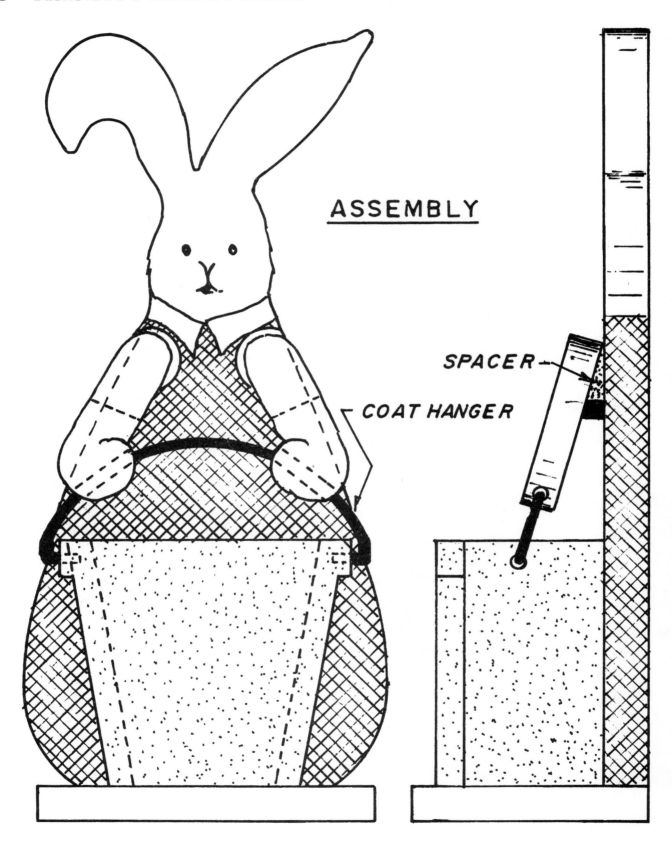

ASSEMBLY

SPACER

COAT HANGER

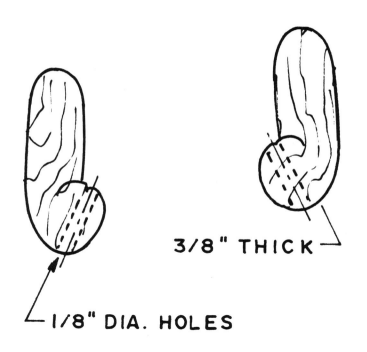

3/8" THICK

1/8" DIA. HOLES

PATTERNS

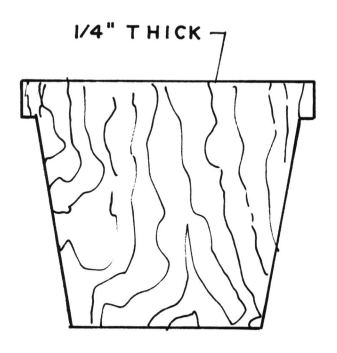

1/4" THICK

BASE: 3/8" X 2 1/2" - 3 1/2" LONG

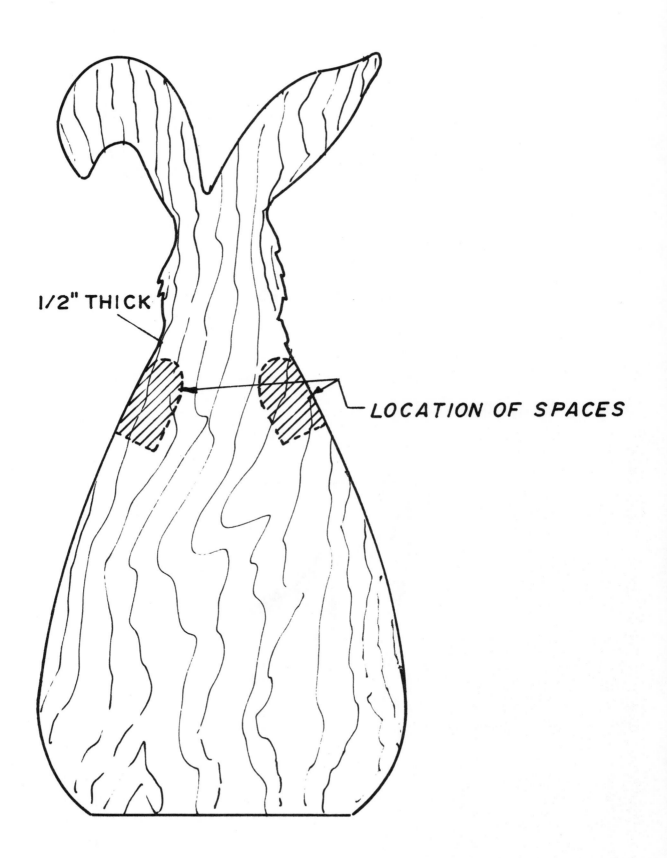

1/2" THICK

LOCATION OF SPACES

14◆Napkin Holder

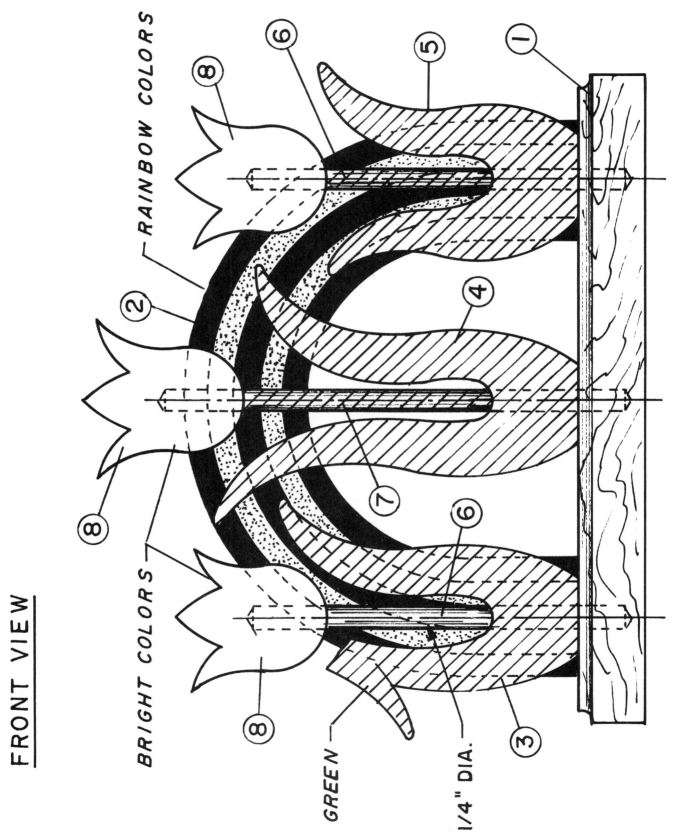

FRONT VIEW

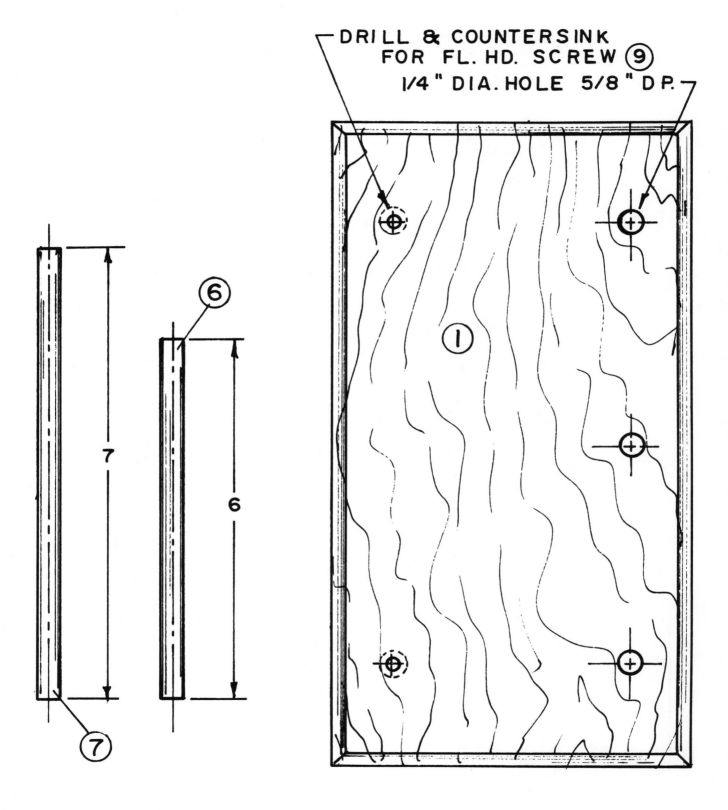

DRILL & COUNTERSINK
FOR FL. HD. SCREW ⑨
1/4" DIA. HOLE 5/8" DP.

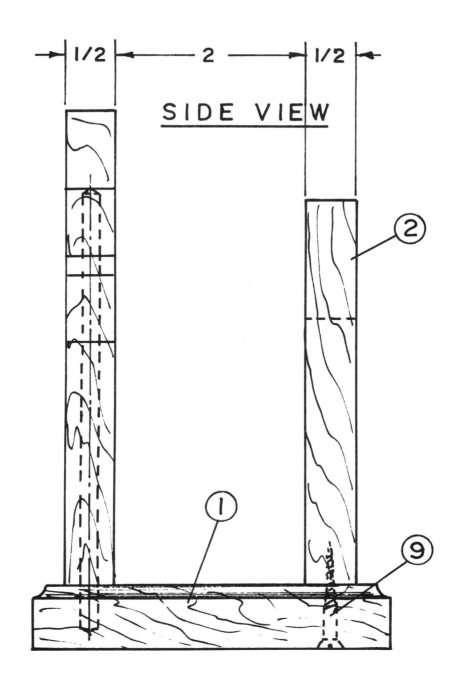

SIDE VIEW

NO.	NAME	SIZE	REQ'D.
1	BASE	3/4 X 3 3/4 - 7 LONG	1
2	RAINBOW	1/2 X 4 1/8 - 6 LONG	1
3	LEAF	1/2 X 2 3/4 - 3 1/4 LG.	1
4	LEAF	1/2 X 2 7/8 - 3 7/8 LG.	1
5	LEAF	1/2 X 2 3/8 - 2 5/8 LG.	1
6	STEM - SHORT	1/4 DIA. - 3 7/8 LONG	2
7	STEM - LONG	1/4 DIA. - 4 7/8 LONG	1
8	FLOWER	1/2 X 1 5/8 - 1 5/8 LG.	3
9	SCREW - FL. HD.	NO. 6 - 1 1/4 LONG	2

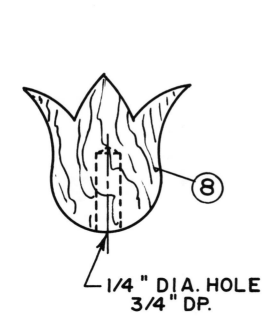

⑧

1/4 " DIA. HOLE
3/4 " DP.

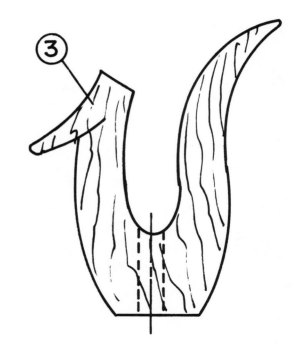

③

PATTERNS

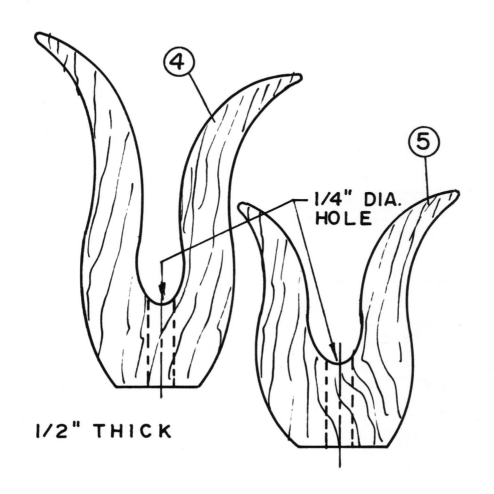

④

⑤

1/4" DIA.
HOLE

1/2" THICK

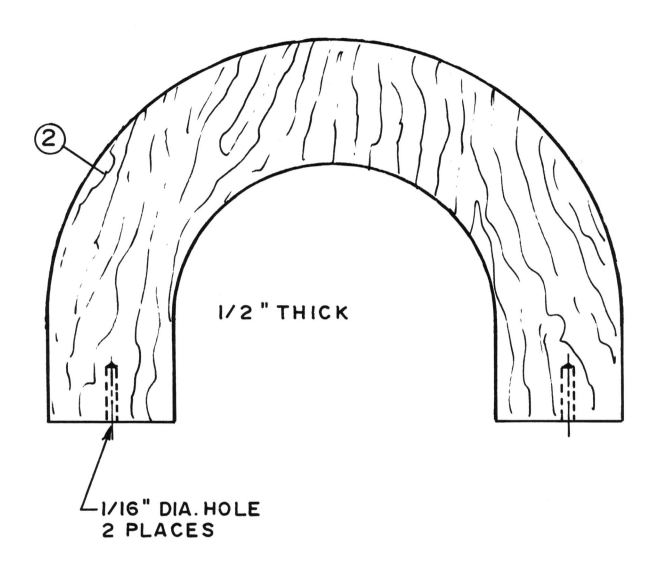

(2)

1/2 " THICK

1/16" DIA. HOLE
2 PLACES

15 ♦ Flower Easter Basket

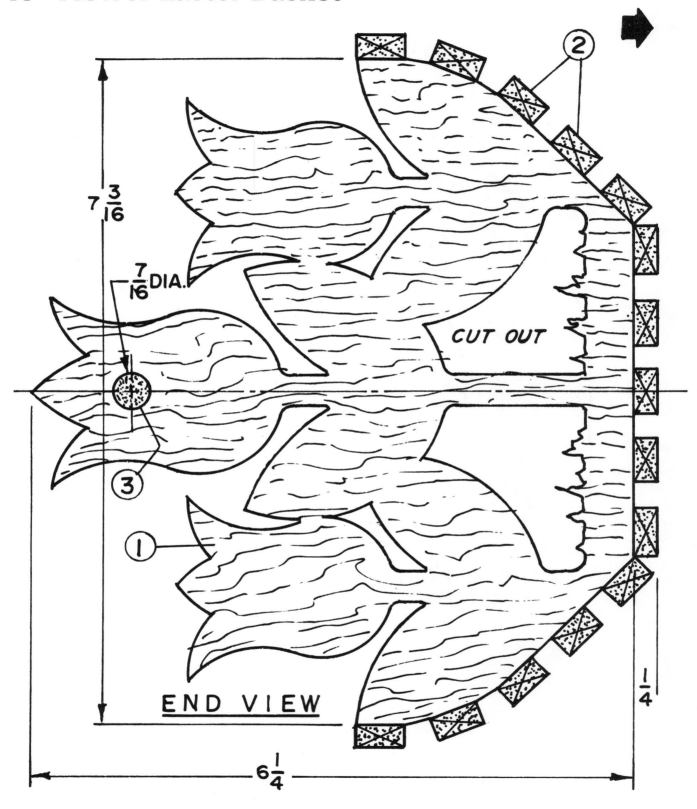

$7\frac{3}{16}$

$\frac{7}{16}$ DIA.

CUT OUT

②

③

①

END VIEW

$6\frac{1}{4}$

$\frac{1}{4}$

FULL-SIZE PATTERN

ASSEMBLE

EXACTLY LIKE

SWAN BASKET

PROJECT 12

NO.	NAME	SIZE	REQ'D.
1	SIDE	1/2 X 6 1/4 - 7 3/16	2
2	END / BOTTOM	1/4 X 1/2 - 6 LONG	15
3	HANDLE	7/16 DIA. X 6 1/4 LG.	1
4	BRAD	3/4 LONG	30

FOURTH OF JULY

16 ♦ Patriotic Bunny

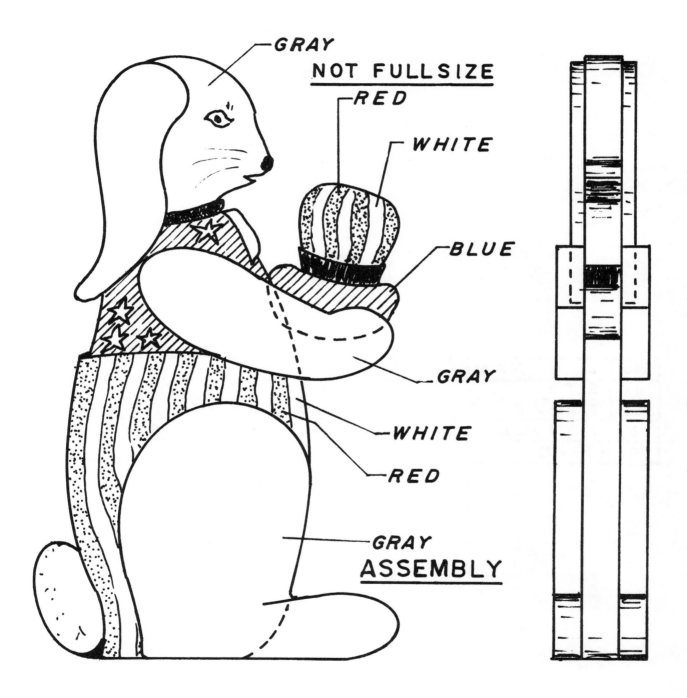

GRAY

NOT FULLSIZE

RED

WHITE

BLUE

GRAY

WHITE

RED

GRAY
ASSEMBLY

EAR
1/8" THICK

HAT
1/2" THICK

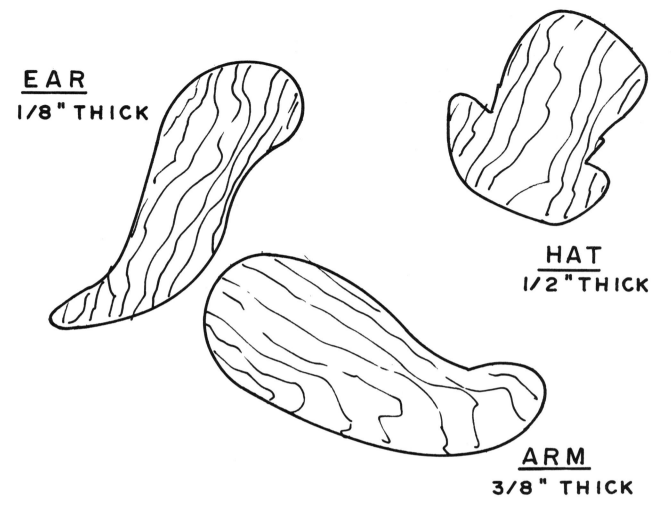

ARM
3/8" THICK

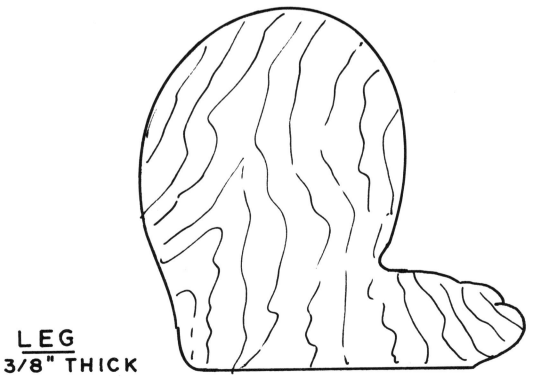

LEG
3/8" THICK

BODY
1/2" THICK

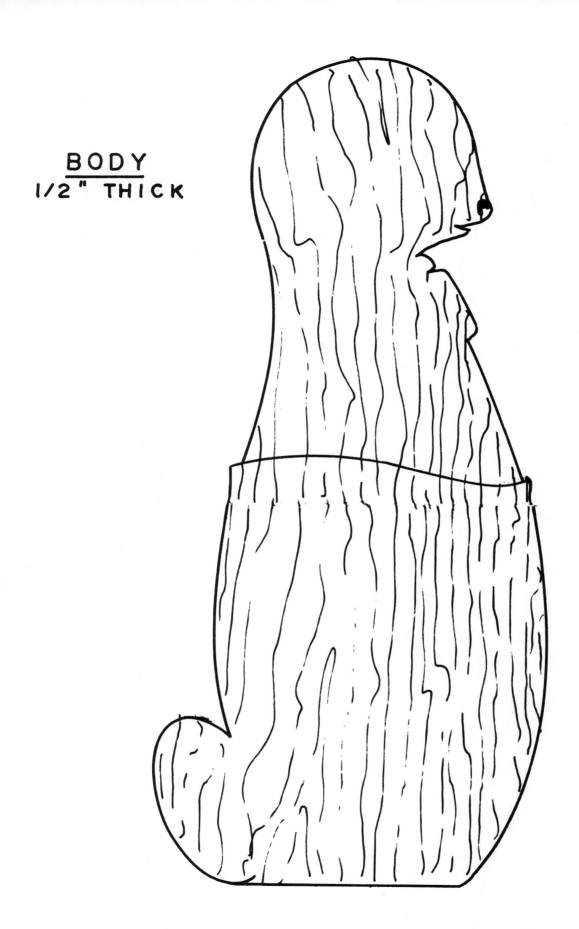

17♦Firecrackers on a Stand

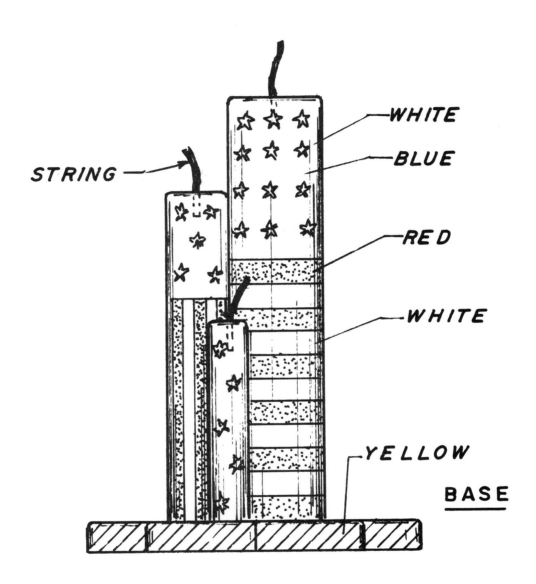

STRING

WHITE

BLUE

RED

WHITE

YELLOW

BASE

SIDE VIEW

PATTERN

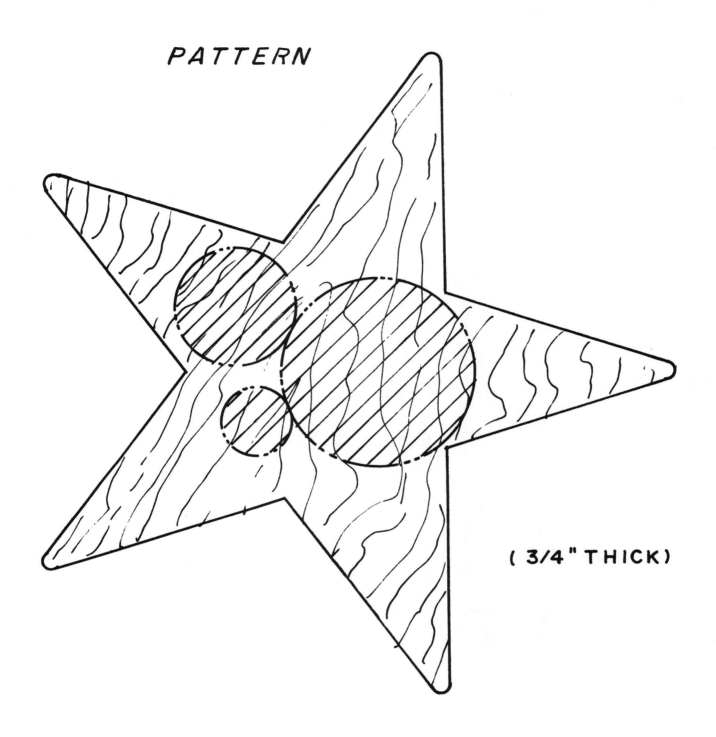

(3/4" THICK)

BASE

TOP VIEW

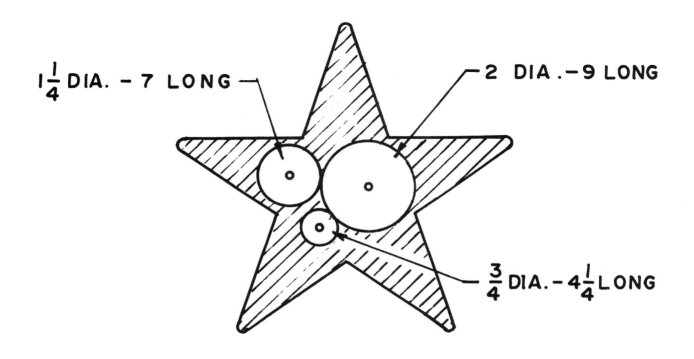

$1\frac{1}{4}$ DIA. - 7 LONG

2 DIA. - 9 LONG

$\frac{3}{4}$ DIA. - $4\frac{1}{4}$ LONG

BASE

18♦Uncle Sam on a Stick

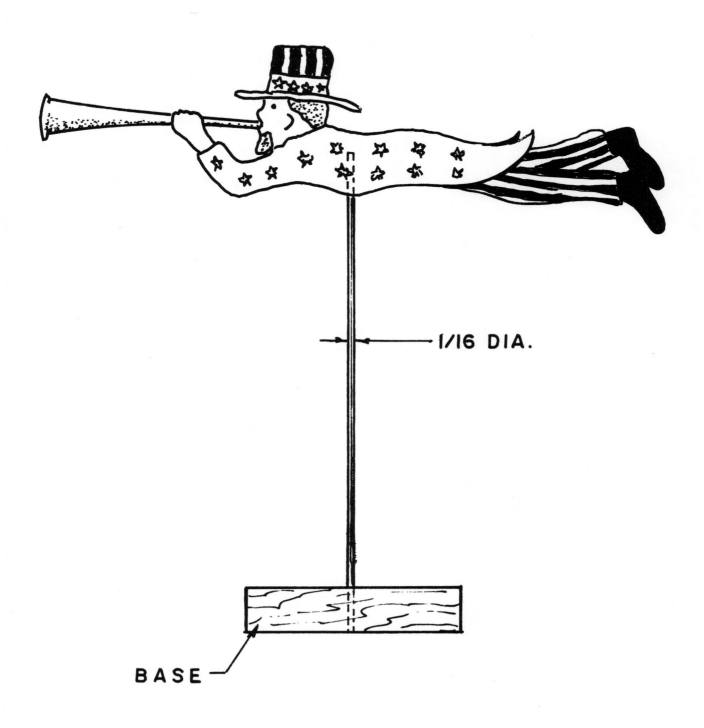

1/16 DIA.

BASE

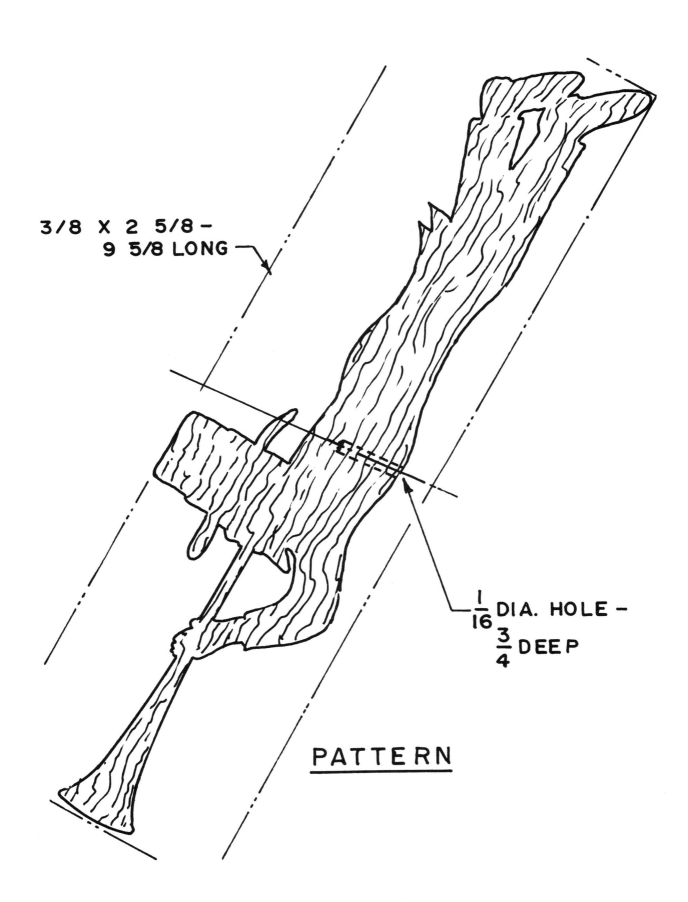

3/8 X 2 5/8 —
9 5/8 LONG

$\frac{1}{16}$ DIA. HOLE —
$\frac{3}{4}$ DEEP

PATTERN

19 ♦ Marching Band

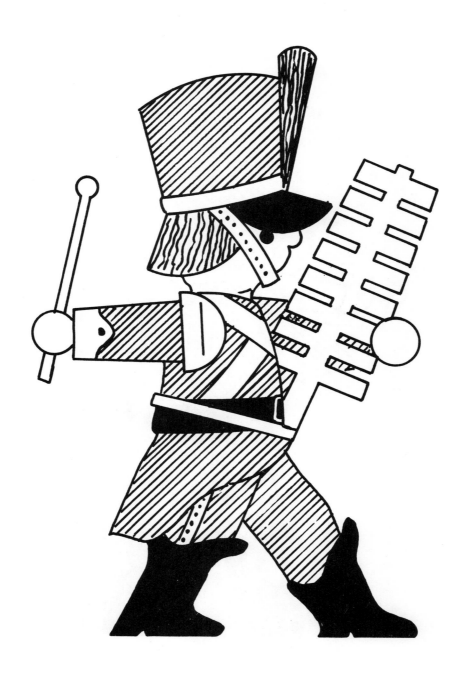

58

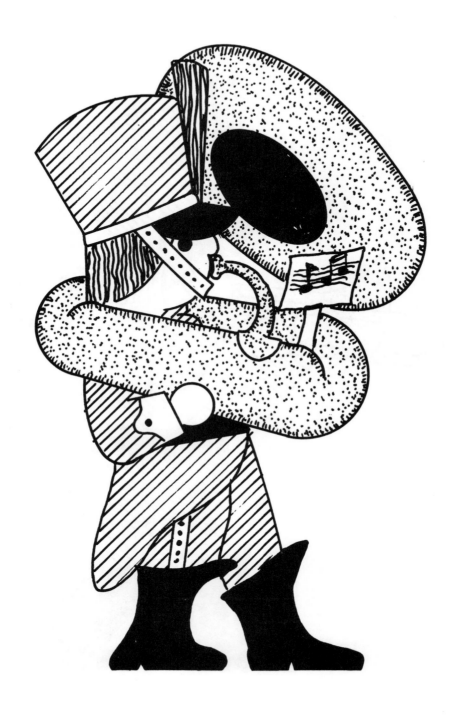

20 ◆ Flag Cart on Wheels

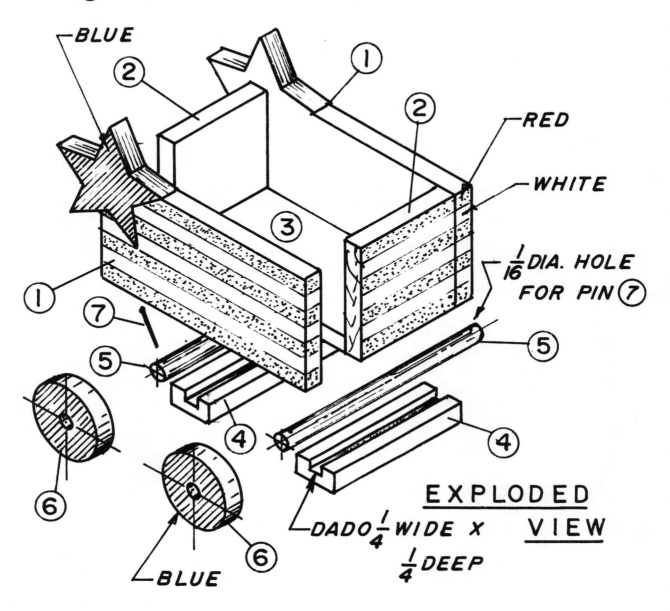

BLUE

RED

WHITE

$\frac{1}{16}$ DIA. HOLE FOR PIN ⑦

DADO $\frac{1}{4}$ WIDE X $\frac{1}{4}$ DEEP

BLUE

E X P L O D E D

V I E W

NO.	NAME	SIZE	REQ'D.
1	SIDE	1/2 X 4 5/8 – 7 7/8	2
2	END	1/2 X 3 1/2 – 3 LG.	2
3	BOTTOM	1/2 X 3 – 5 1/2 LG.	1
4	SUPPORT	1/2 X 1 – 4 LONG	2
5	AXLE	1/4 X 5 1/2 LONG	2
6	WHEEL	2 DIA. X 1/2 TK.	4
7	PIN	TO SUIT	4

27 *Dancing Pumpkins with Candles*

24 Stick Projects

29 *Witch Basket;*
22 *German Folk Art Witch, circa 1935*

A

52 *Happy Birthday Clown*

10 *Leprechaun on Clover Stand*

31 *Indian/Pilgrim Silhouette, circa 1935; 30 Pilgrim Silhouette*

38 *Evergreen Trees on a Stick;* 46 *Rocking Santa on a Stand;* 51 *Toy Train with Four Cars;* 43 *Toy Sled*

42 *String Projects;* 48 *Signs of the Seasons*

34 *Snowmen*

5 Angel on a Shelf; 6 Wall Box with
Hearts; 2 Love Birds; 7 "I Love You" Sign

15 Flower Easter Basket; 14 Napkin Holder

13 Rabbit Plant Holder; 12 Swan Easter Basket;
11 Easter Bunny

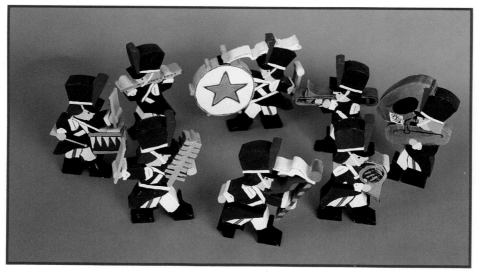

19 Marching Band

D

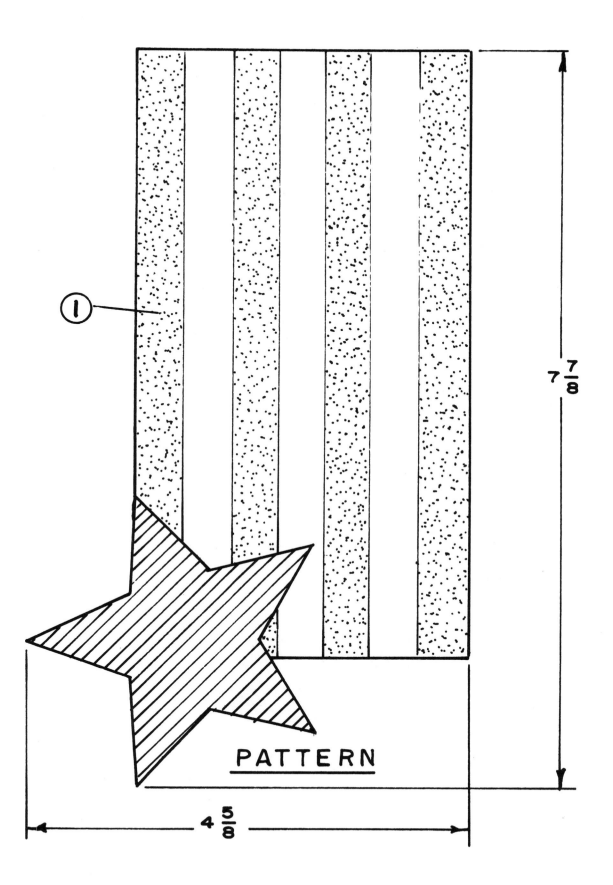

①

PATTERN

$7\frac{7}{8}$

$4\frac{5}{8}$

21◆Pig Cutting Board

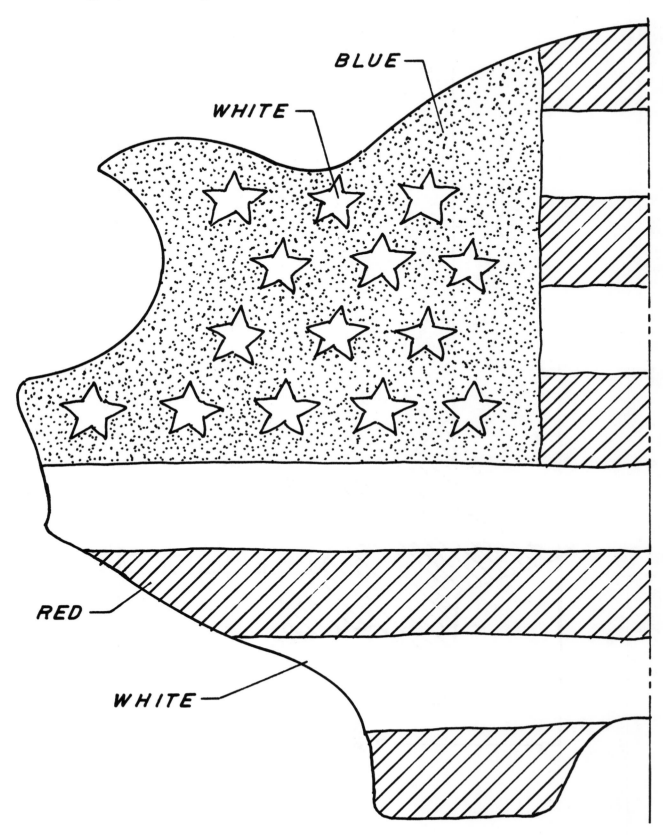

BLUE

WHITE

RED

WHITE

66

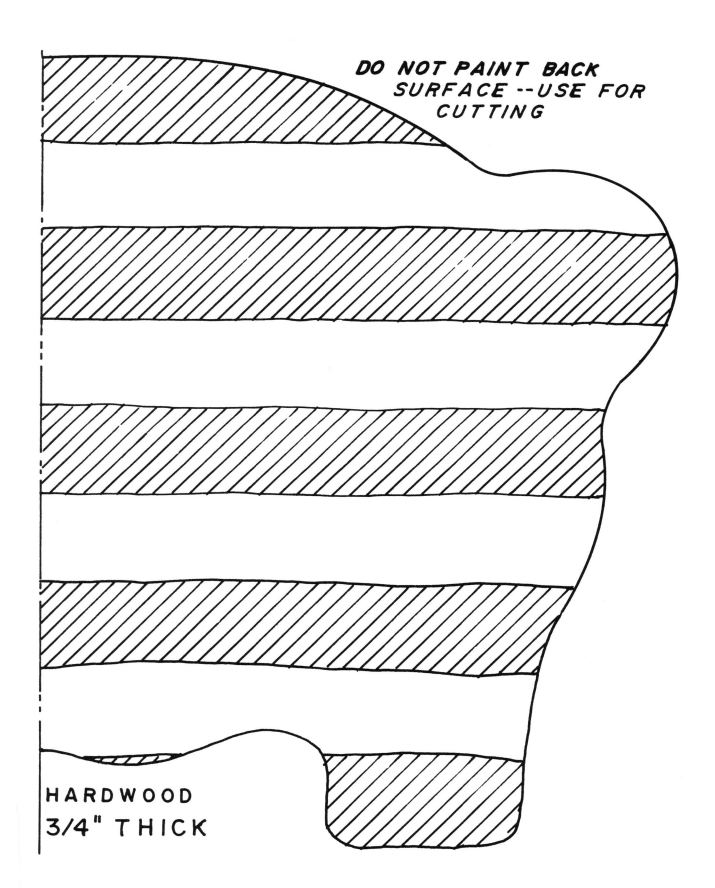

DO NOT PAINT BACK
SURFACE --USE FOR
CUTTING

HARDWOOD
3/4" THICK

HALLOWEEN

22◆German Folk Art Witch, circa 1935

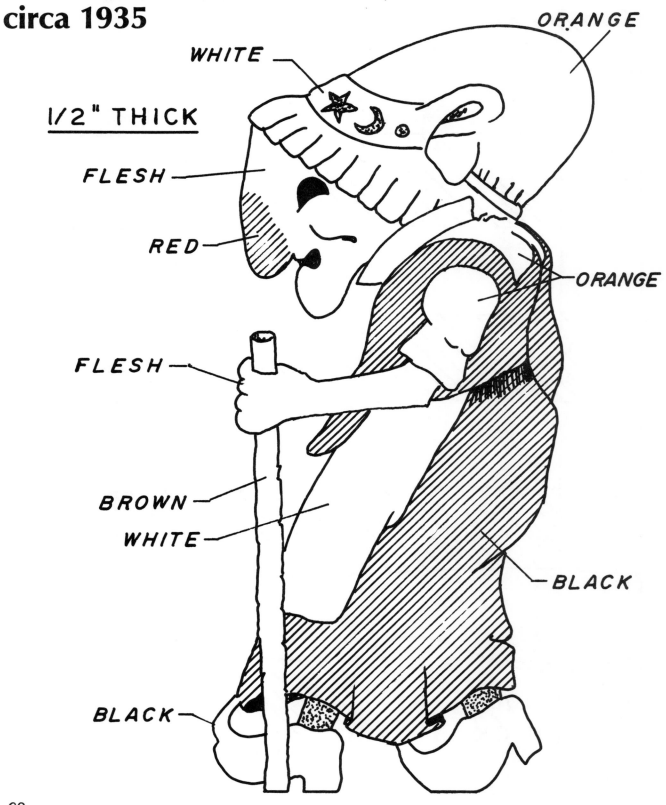

WHITE

ORANGE

1/2" THICK

FLESH

RED

FLESH

ORANGE

BROWN

WHITE

BLACK

BLACK

23 ◆ Stick Projects

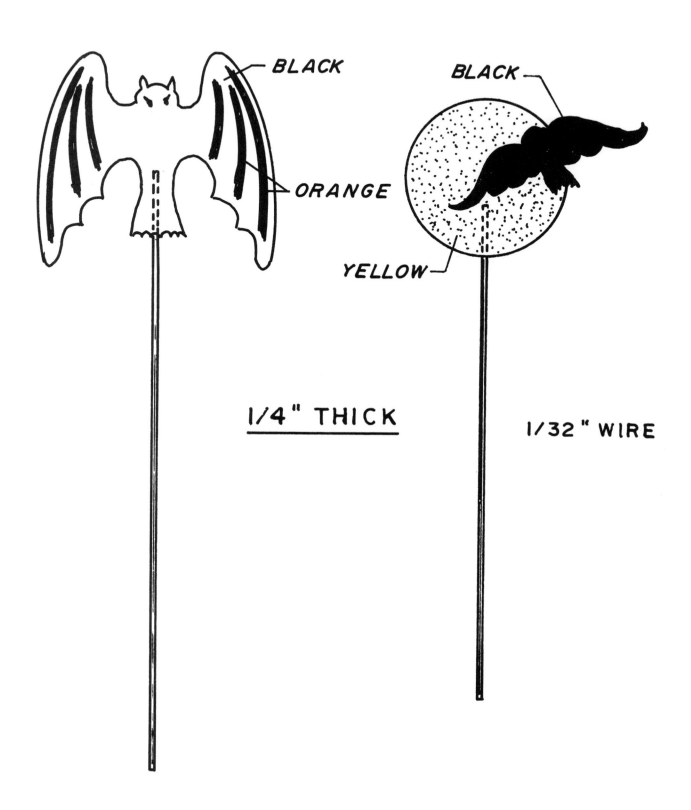

BLACK

BLACK

ORANGE

YELLOW

1/4" THICK

1/32" WIRE

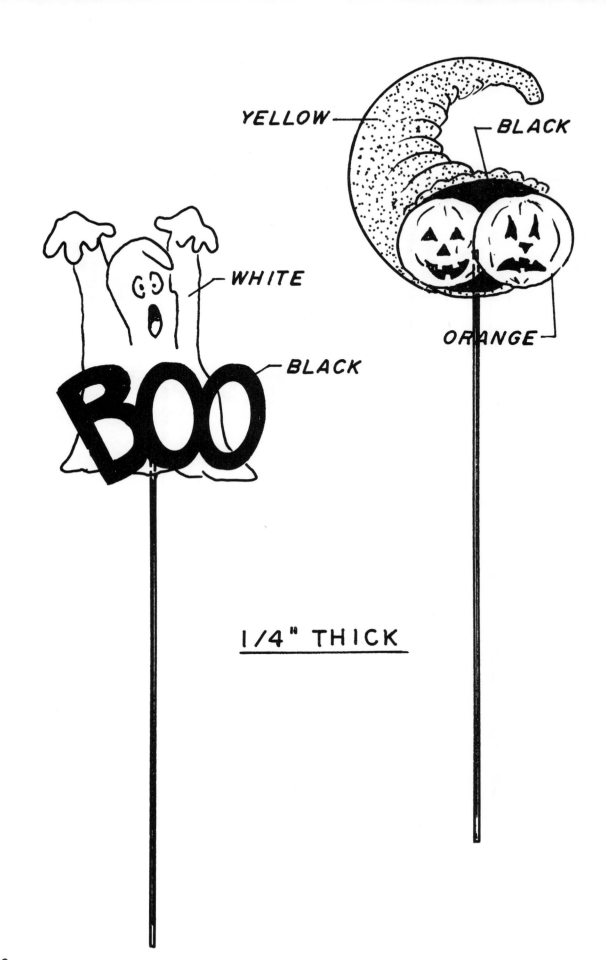

YELLOW

BLACK

WHITE

BLACK

ORANGE

1/4" THICK

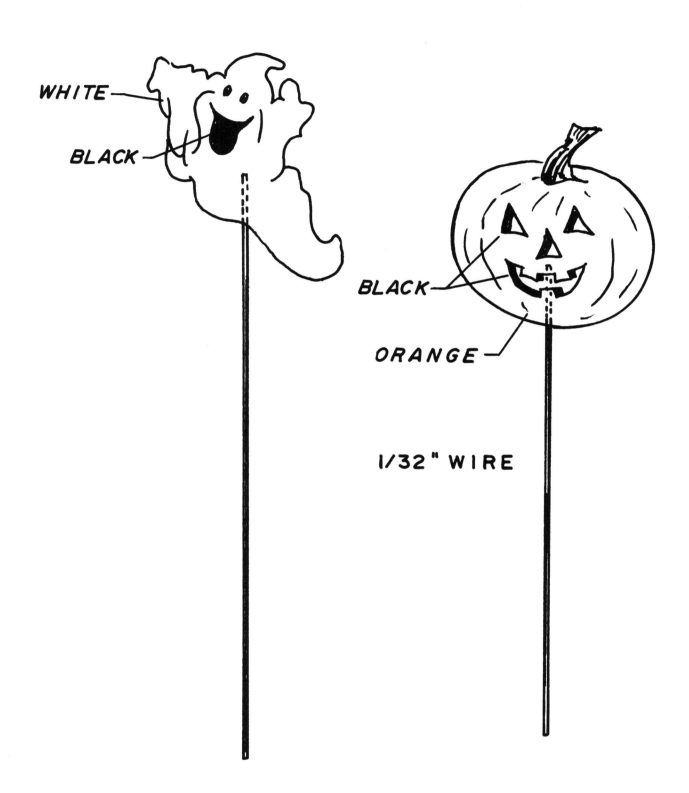

WHITE

BLACK

BLACK

ORANGE

1/32" WIRE

STRING

1/4" THICK

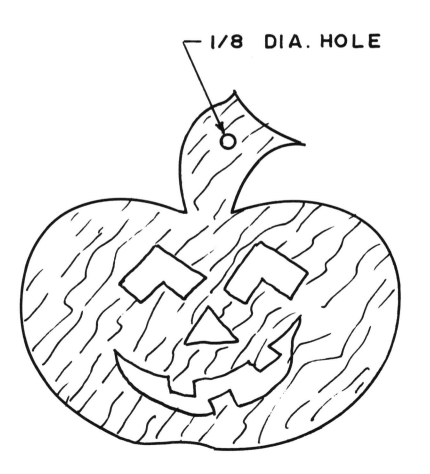

1/8 DIA. HOLE

PAINT BLACK

25 ◆ Flying Witch

ENLARGE TO 1" GRID

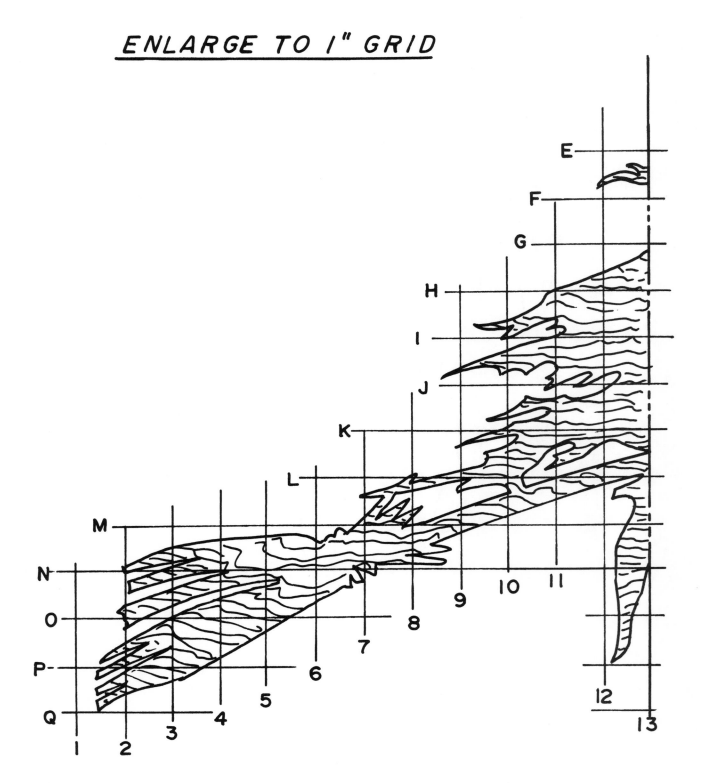

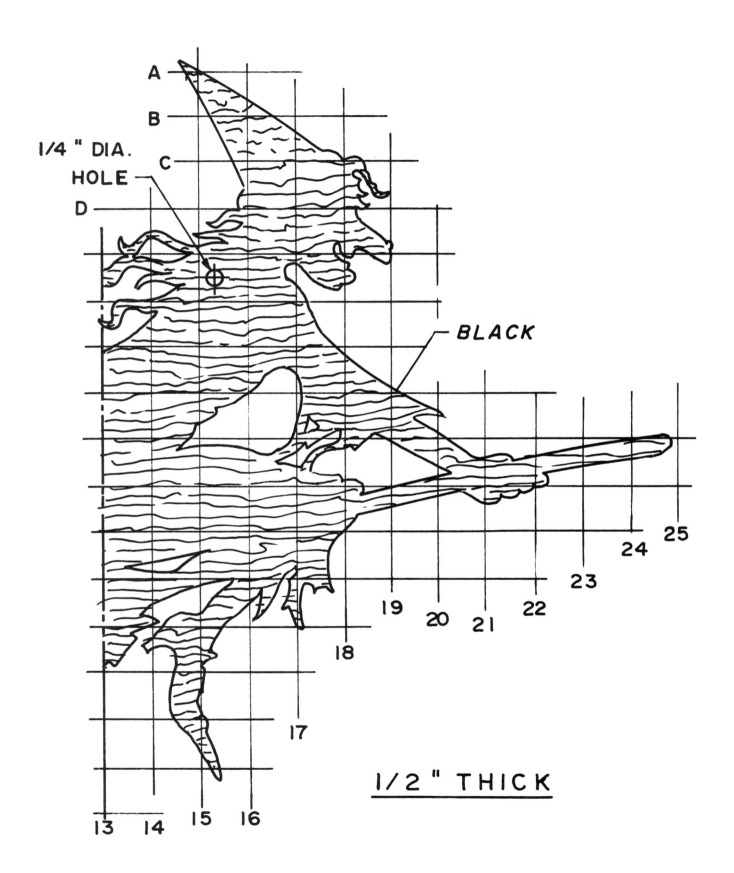

A

B

1/4 " DIA.
HOLE   C

D

BLACK

1/2 " THICK

13   14   15   16   17   18   19   20   21   22   23   24   25

26♦Chain of Ghosts

ALL NOTCHES 3/8" WIDE

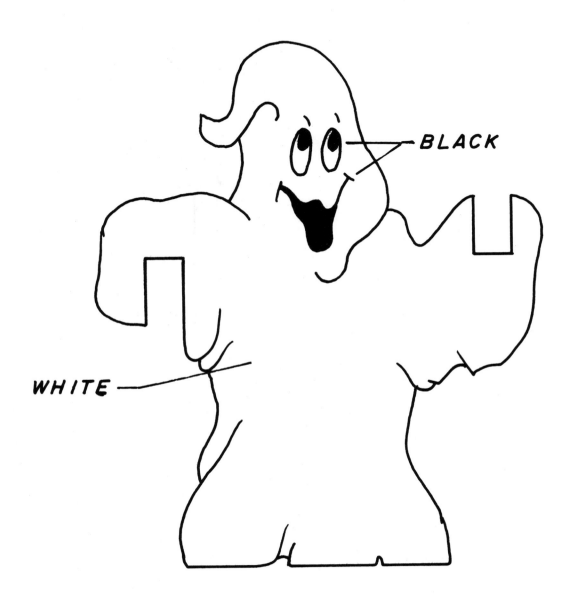

BLACK

WHITE

1/4" THICK

82

27♦Dancing Pumpkins with Candles

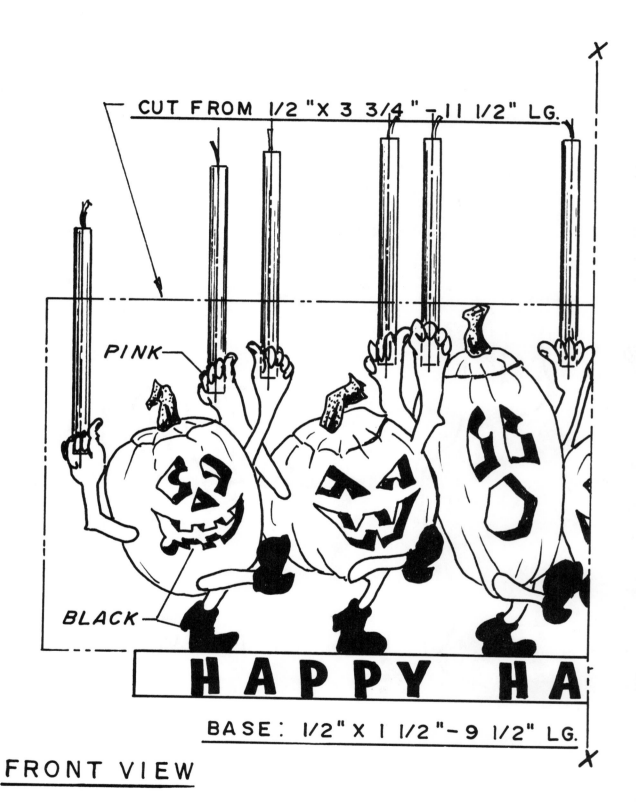

CUT FROM 1/2"x 3 3/4" - 11 1/2" LG.

PINK

BLACK

HAPPY HA

BASE: 1/2" x 1 1/2" - 9 1/2" LG.

FRONT VIEW

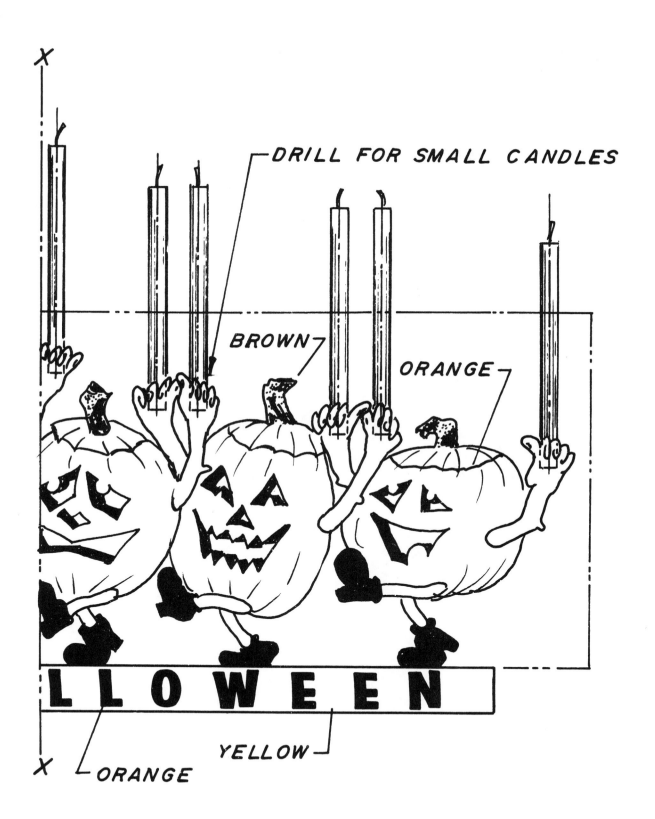

DRILL FOR SMALL CANDLES

BROWN

ORANGE

LLOWEEN

ORANGE

YELLOW

28 ◆ Ghosts Basket

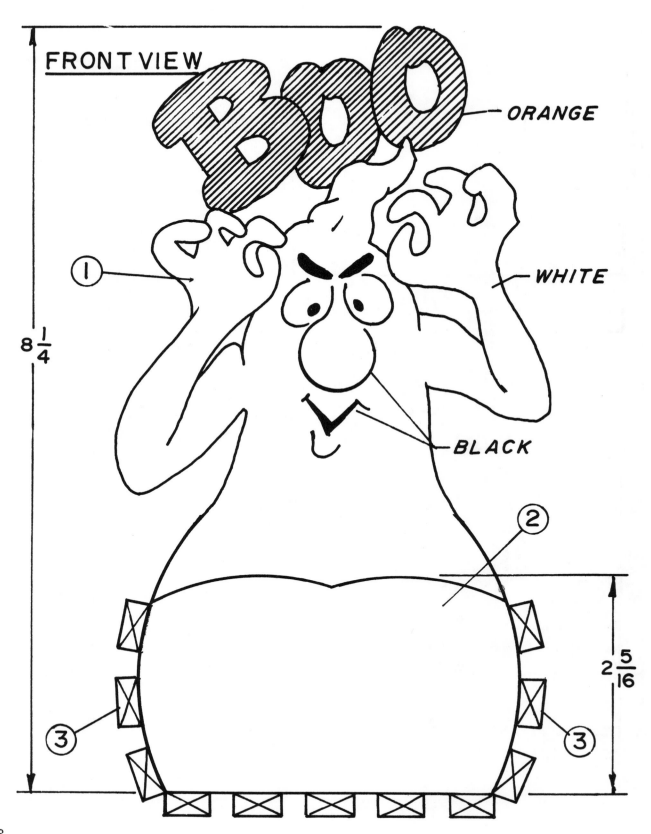

FRONT VIEW

BOO

ORANGE

WHITE

BLACK

$8\frac{1}{4}$

$2\frac{5}{16}$

①

②

③

③

SIDE VIEW

NO.	NAME	SIZE	REQ'D
1	BACK	1/2 X 4 5/8 - 8 1/4 LG.	1
2	FRONT	1/2 X 2 5/16 - 4 LONG	1
3	SIDE	1/4 X 1/2 - 6 1/2 LG.	11
4	BRAD	3/4 LONG	44

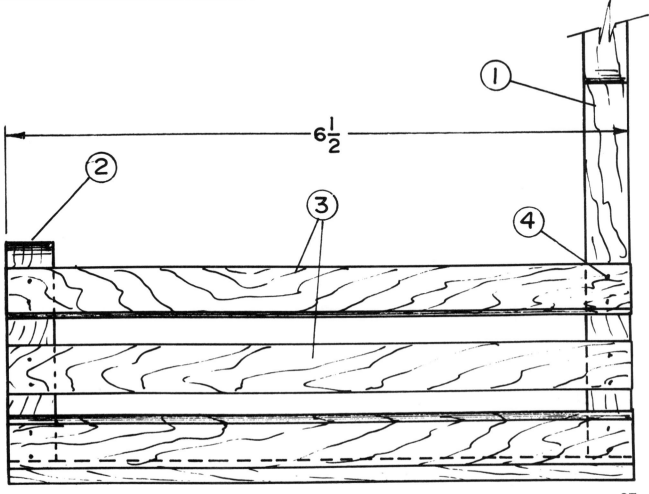

29♦Witch Basket

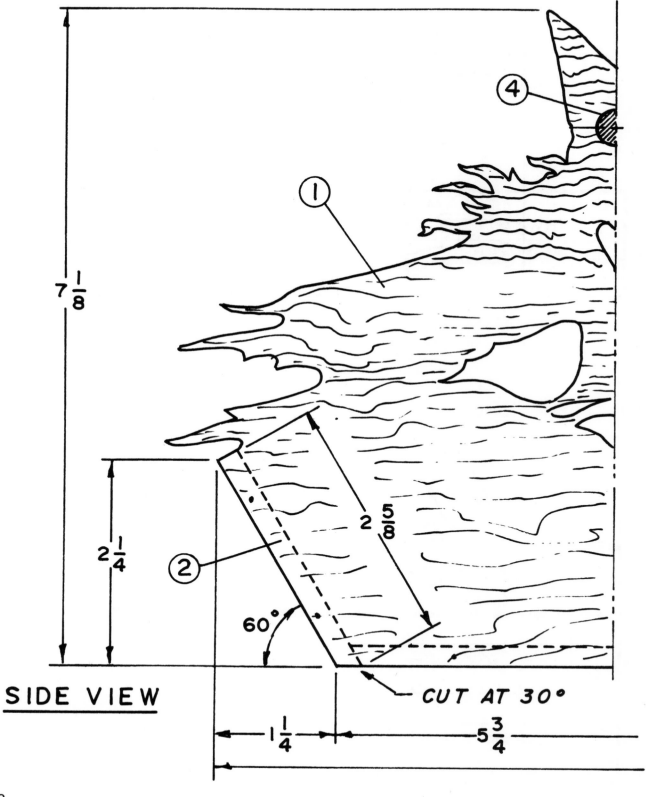

SIDE VIEW

CUT AT 30°

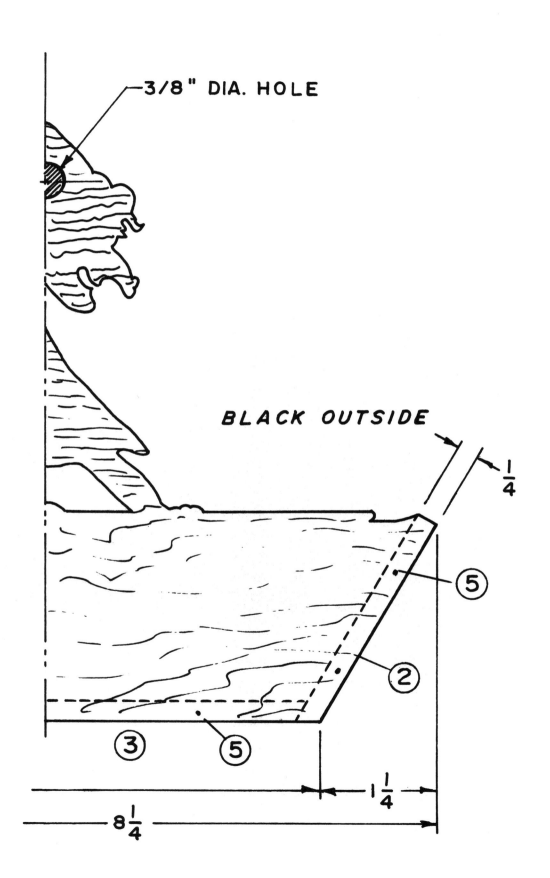

3/8" DIA. HOLE

BLACK OUTSIDE

¼

⑤

②

③ ⑤

1¼

8¼

NO.	NAME	SIZE	REQ'D.
1	SIDE	3/8 X 7 1/8 – 8 1/4 LG.	2
2	END	1/4 X 2 5/8 – 5 1/4 LG.	2
3	BOTTOM	1/4 X 5 1/4 – 5 5/8 LG.	1
4	HANDLE	3/8 DIA. X 6 1/4 LG.	1
5	BRAD	3/4 LONG	16

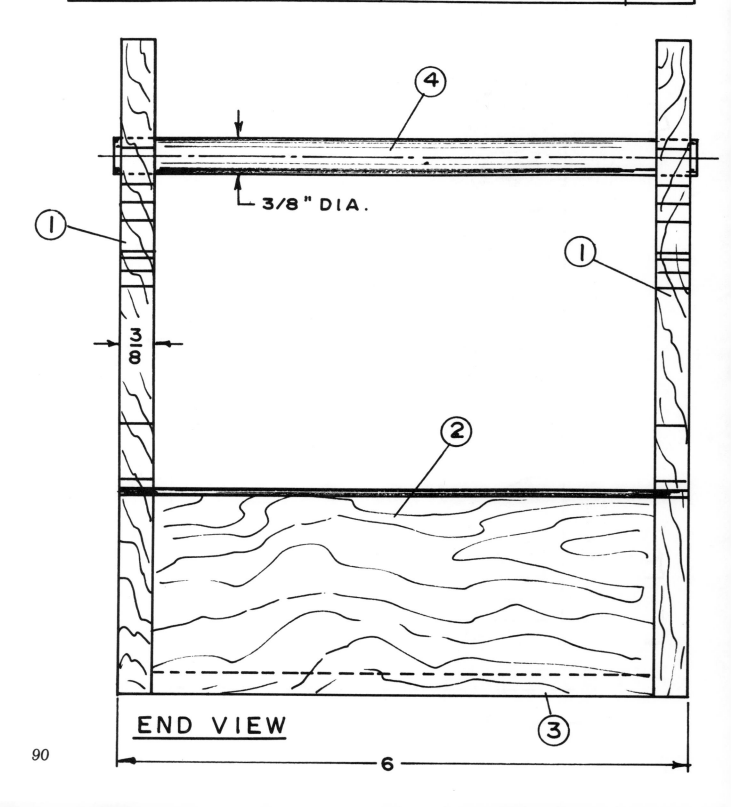

3/8" DIA.

3/8

END VIEW

6

THANKSGIVING

30 ◆ Pilgrim Silhouette

$6\frac{1}{2}$

31♦Indian/Pilgrim Silhouette, circa 1935

3/4" THICK

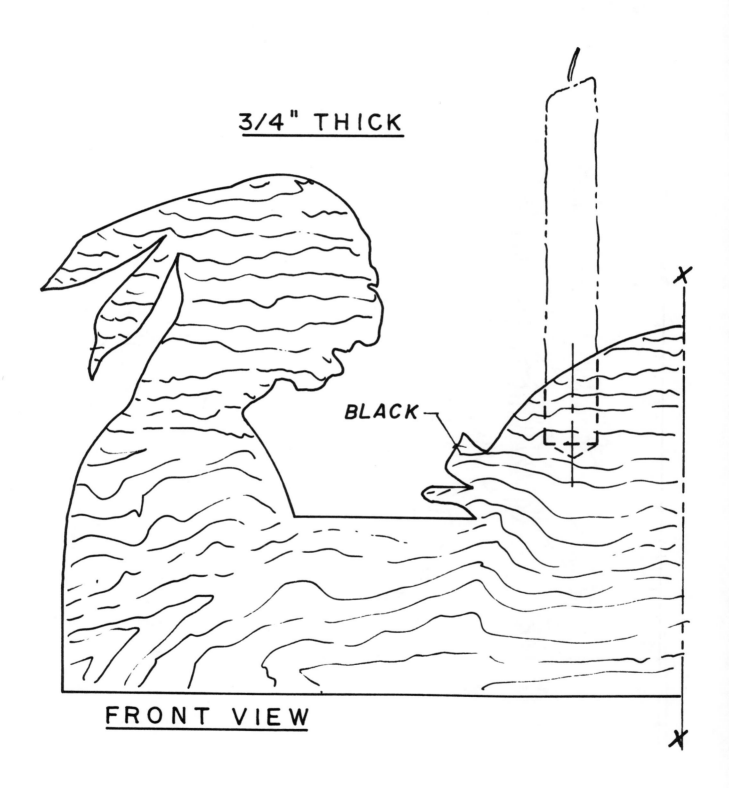

BLACK

FRONT VIEW

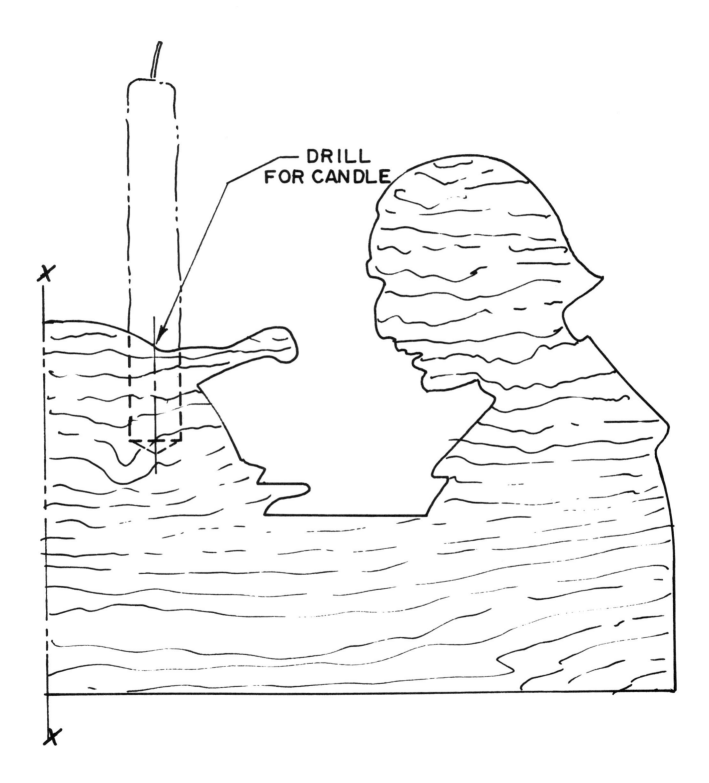

DRILL
FOR CANDLE

X

X

93

32♦Deer Candle Holder

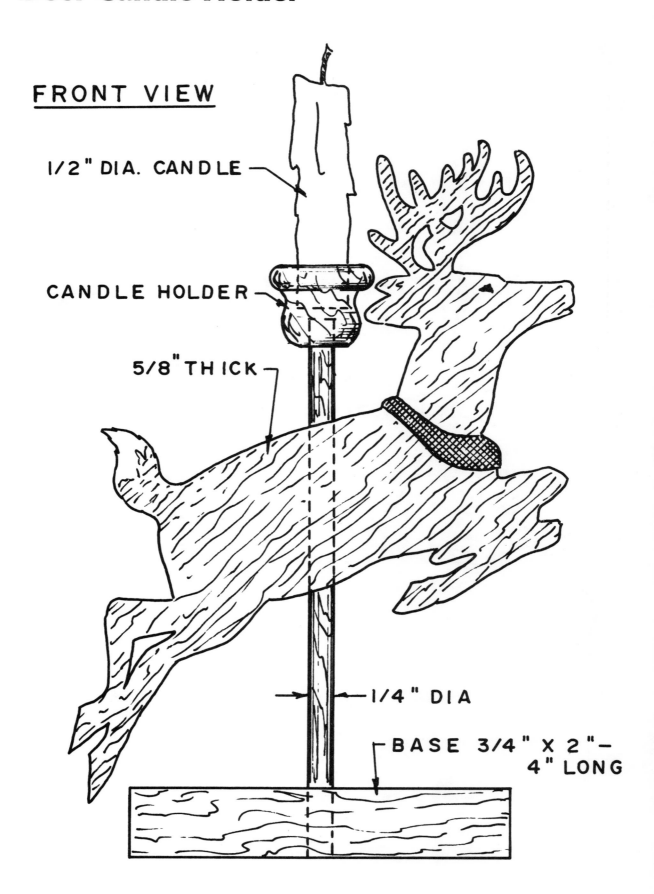

FRONT VIEW

1/2" DIA. CANDLE

CANDLE HOLDER

5/8" THICK

1/4" DIA

BASE 3/4" X 2" —
4" LONG

WINTER HOLIDAYS

33◆Happy Holiday Hobbyhorse

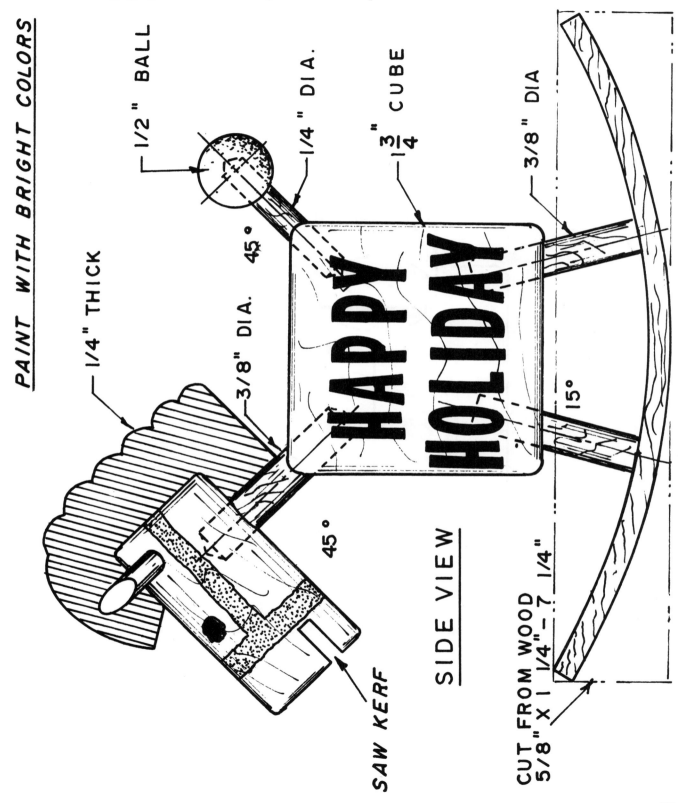

PAINT WITH BRIGHT COLORS

1/2" BALL

1/4" DIA.

1 3/4" CUBE

3/8" DIA

1/4" THICK

3/8" DIA.

45°

45°

15°

SAW KERF

SIDE VIEW

CUT FROM WOOD
5/8" X 1 1/4" – 7 1/4"

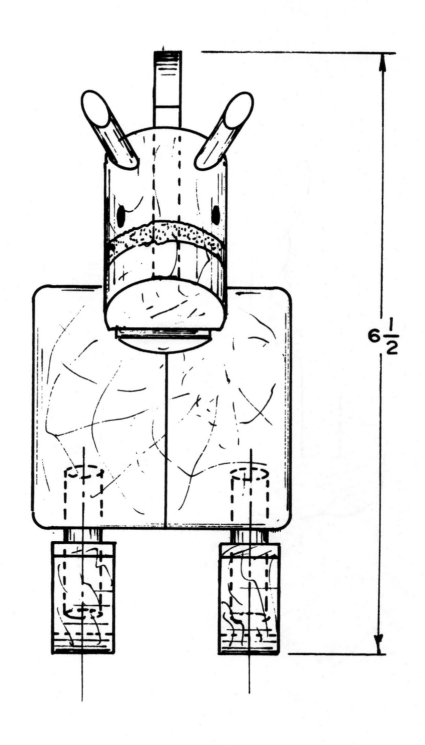

$6\frac{1}{2}$

<u>F R O N T</u>
<u>VIEW</u>

34 ◆ Snowmen

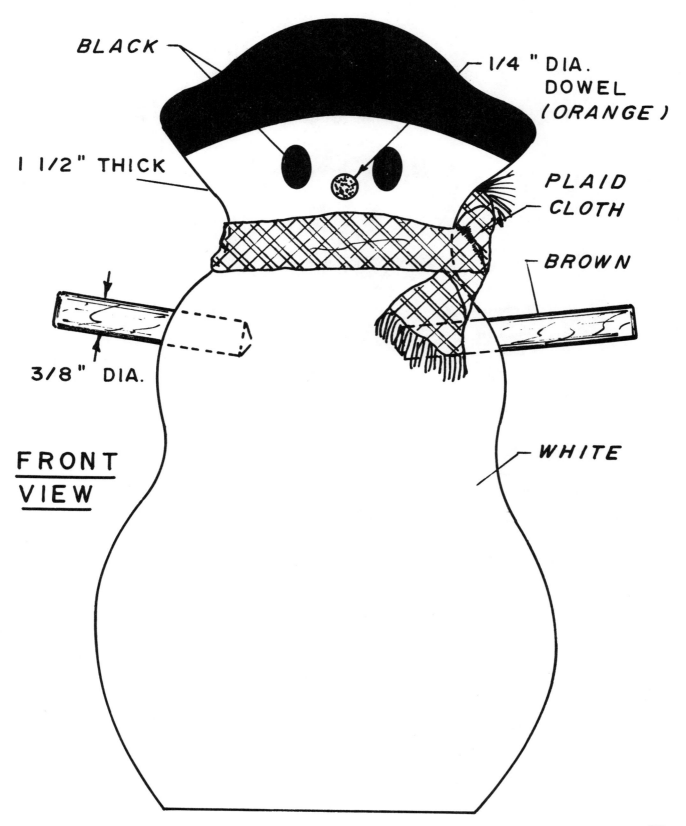

BLACK

1/4" DIA.
DOWEL
(ORANGE)

1 1/2" THICK

PLAID
CLOTH

BROWN

3/8" DIA.

WHITE

FRONT
VIEW

PAINT TO MATCH
LARGE SNOWMAN

1/4" DIA.
DOWEL

5/16" DIA

I 1/2 "
THICK

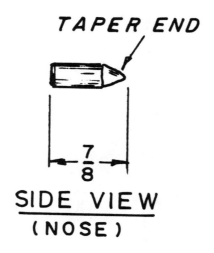

TAPER END

SIDE VIEW
(NOSE)

$\frac{7}{8}$

FRONT VIEW

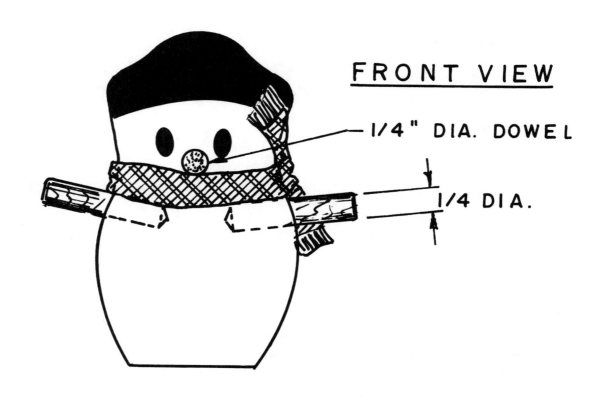

1/4" DIA. DOWEL

1/4 DIA.

35 ♦ Horse Pull Toy

PATTERN

PAINT WITH
BRIGHT COLORS

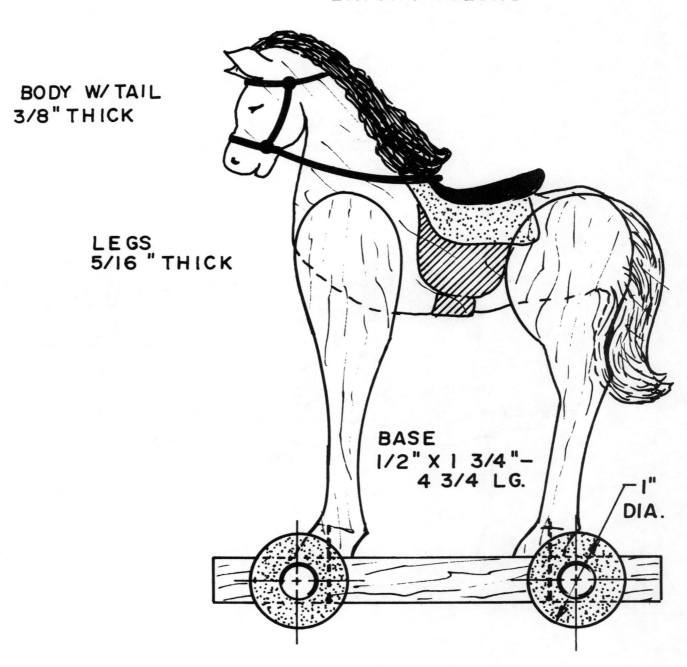

BODY W/TAIL
3/8" THICK

LEGS
5/16" THICK

BASE
1/2" X 1 3/4"–
4 3/4 LG.

1"
DIA.

SIDE VIEW

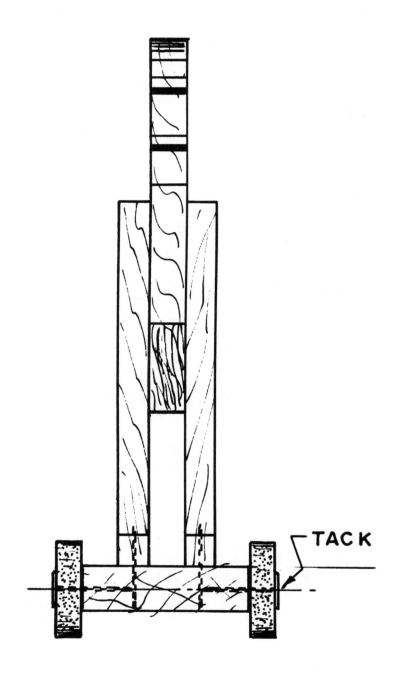

TACK

FRONT VIEW

36 ♦ Rocking Reindeer

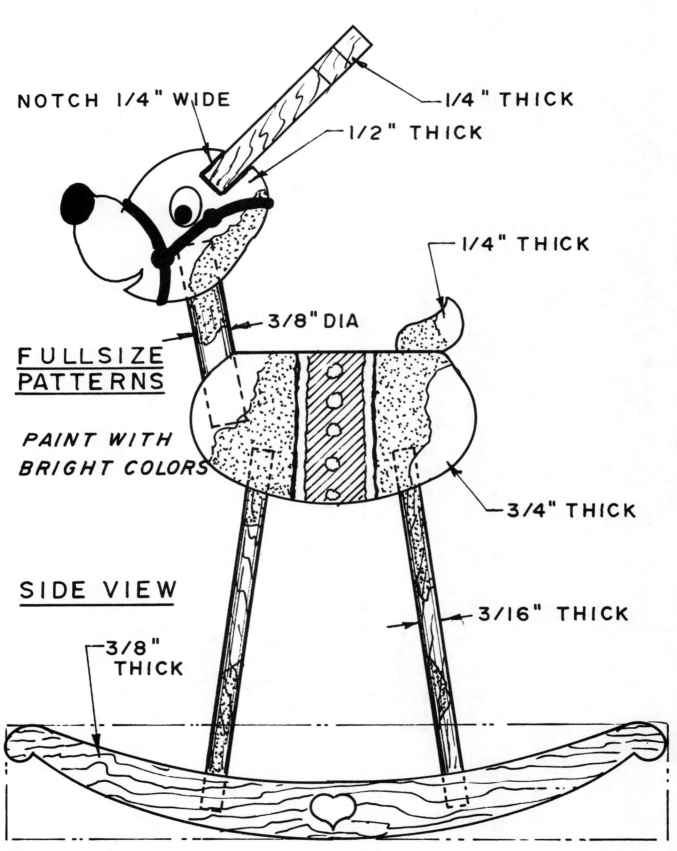

NOTCH 1/4" WIDE

1/4" THICK

1/2" THICK

1/4" THICK

3/8" DIA

FULLSIZE
PATTERNS

PAINT WITH
BRIGHT COLORS

3/4" THICK

SIDE VIEW

3/16" THICK

3/8"
THICK

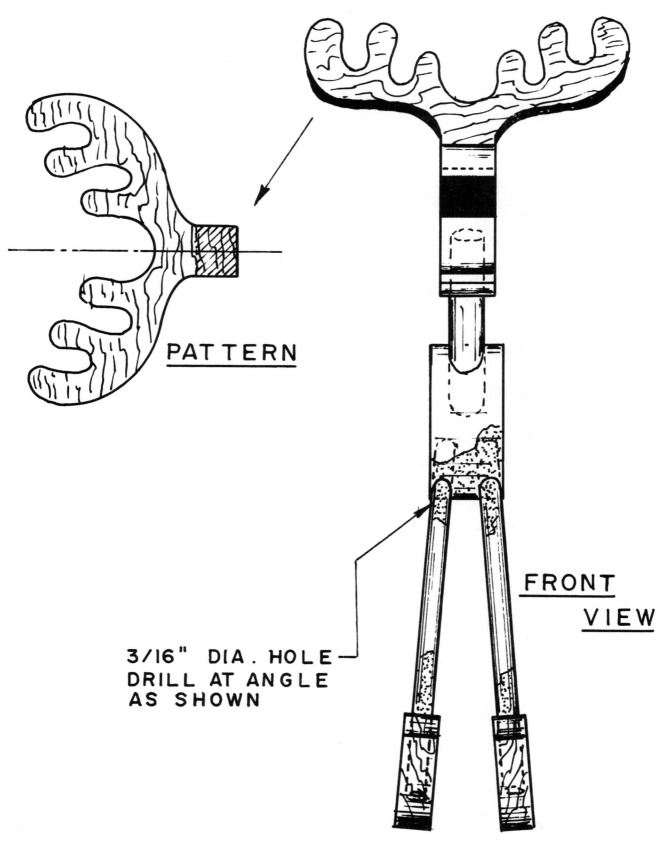

PATTERN

FRONT
VIEW

3/16" DIA. HOLE
DRILL AT ANGLE
AS SHOWN

37♦Snowman

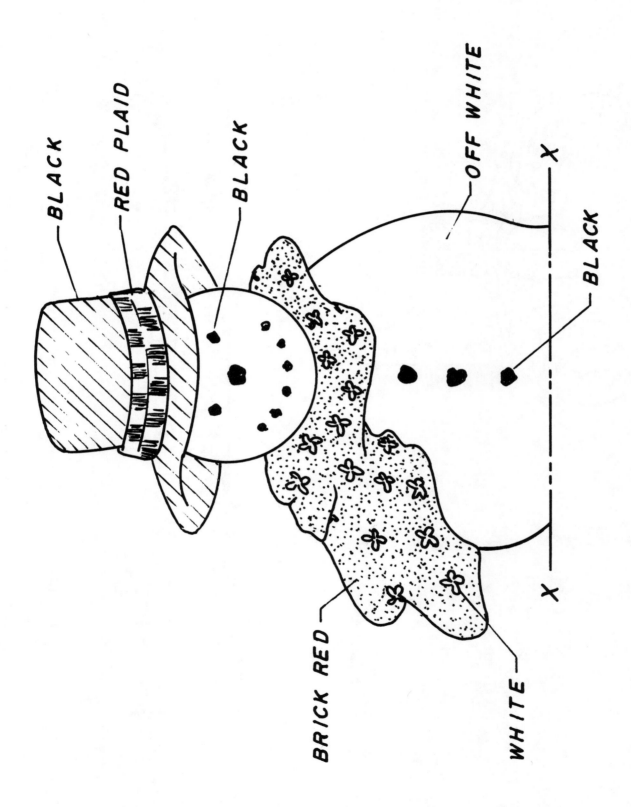

104

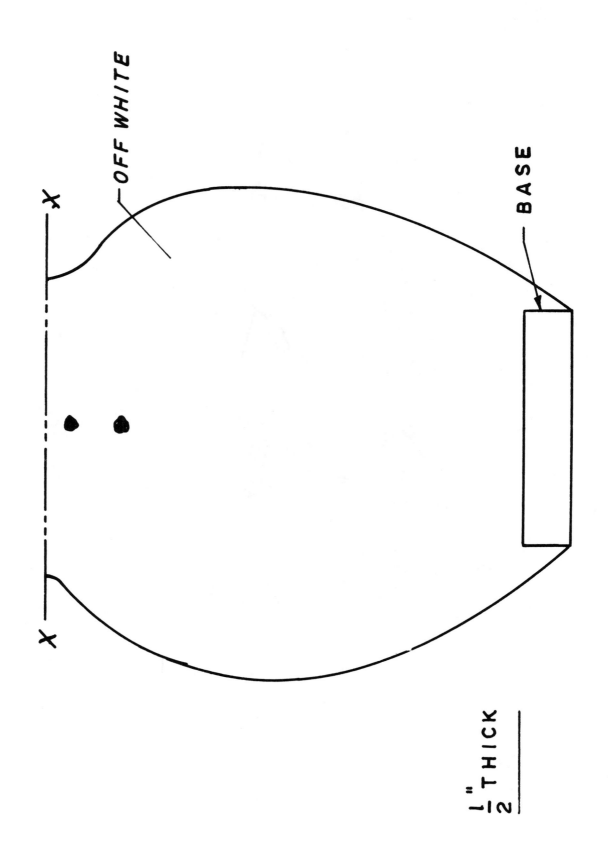

OFF WHITE

X — X

BASE

$\dfrac{1}{2}''$ THICK

105

38◆Evergreen Trees on a Stick

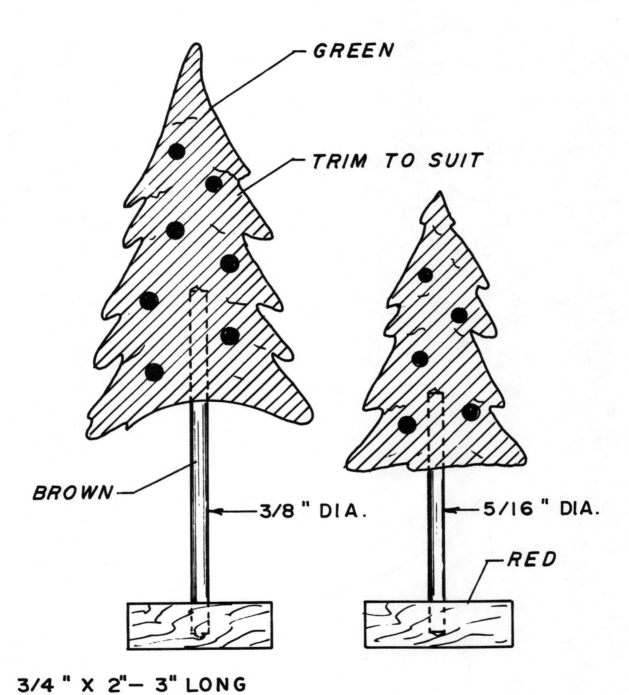

GREEN

TRIM TO SUIT

BROWN

3/8 " DIA.

5/16 " DIA.

RED

3/4 " X 2"– 3" LONG

PATTERN

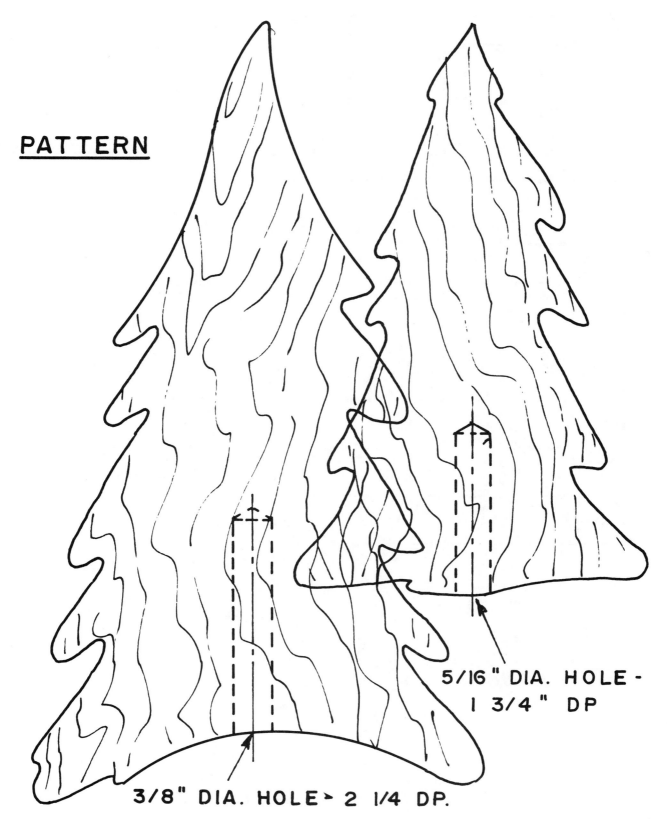

5/16" DIA. HOLE -
I 3/4" DP

3/8" DIA. HOLE - 2 I/4 DP.

39 ◆ Candy Cane Ladder

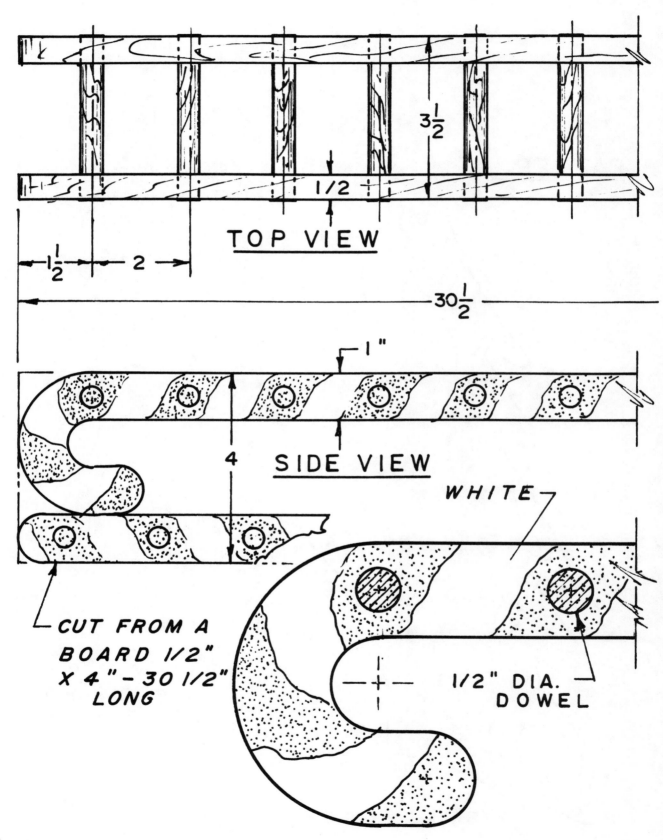

TOP VIEW

$3\frac{1}{2}$

$1/2$

$1\frac{1}{2}$

2

$30\frac{1}{2}$

1"

SIDE VIEW

4

WHITE

CUT FROM A
BOARD 1/2"
X 4" - 30 1/2"
LONG

1/2" DIA.
DOWEL

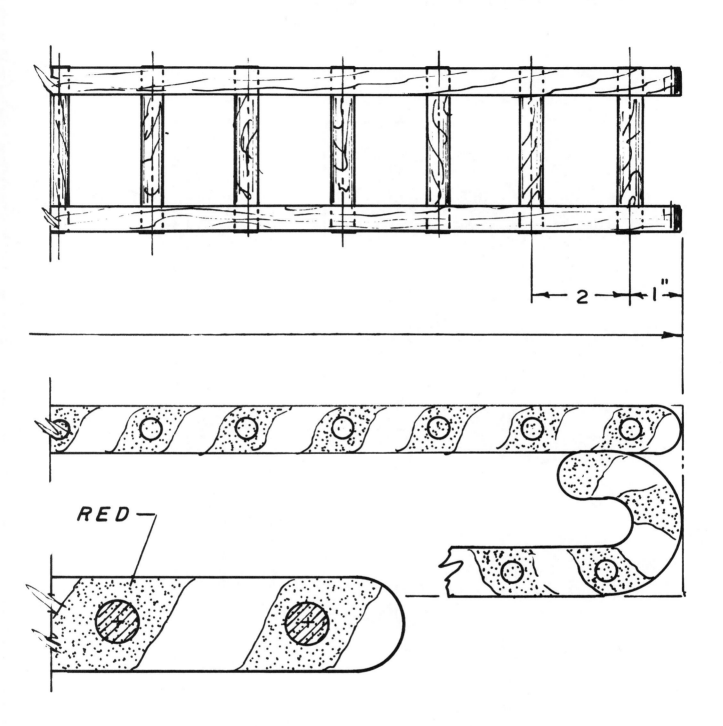

RED

FULL-SIZE PATTERN

40 ◆ Santa-in-Chimney Card Holder

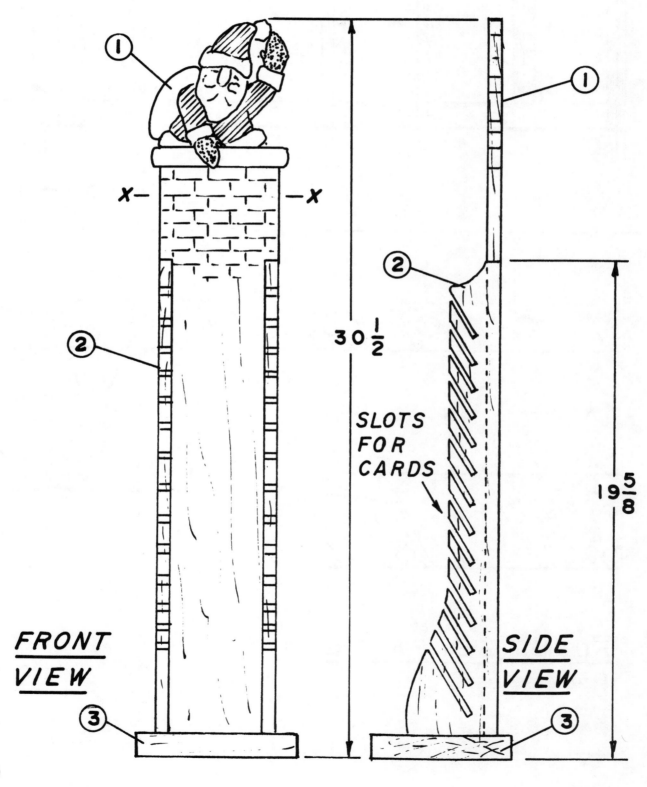

X—   —X

30 $\frac{1}{2}$

SLOTS
FOR
CARDS

19 $\frac{5}{8}$

FRONT VIEW

SIDE VIEW

FULL-SIZE PATTERN

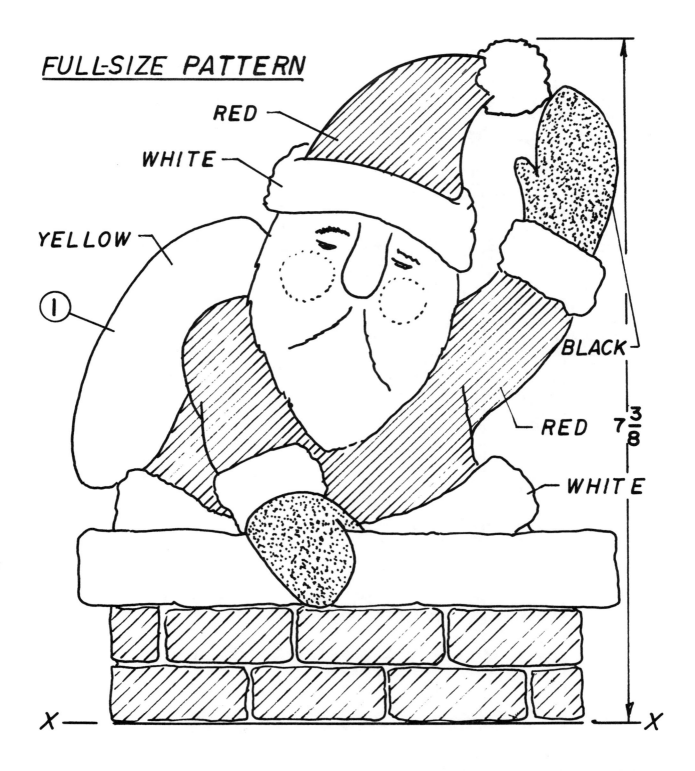

RED

WHITE

YELLOW

①

BLACK

RED

WHITE

$7\frac{3}{8}$

X ——

—— X

NO.	NAME	SIZE	REQD.
1	BACK	1/2 X 5 5/8 – 30 LONG	1
2	SIDE	1/2 X 3 1/2 – 19 5/8 LG.	2
3	BASE	1/2 X 5 5/8 – 6 1/2 LG.	1

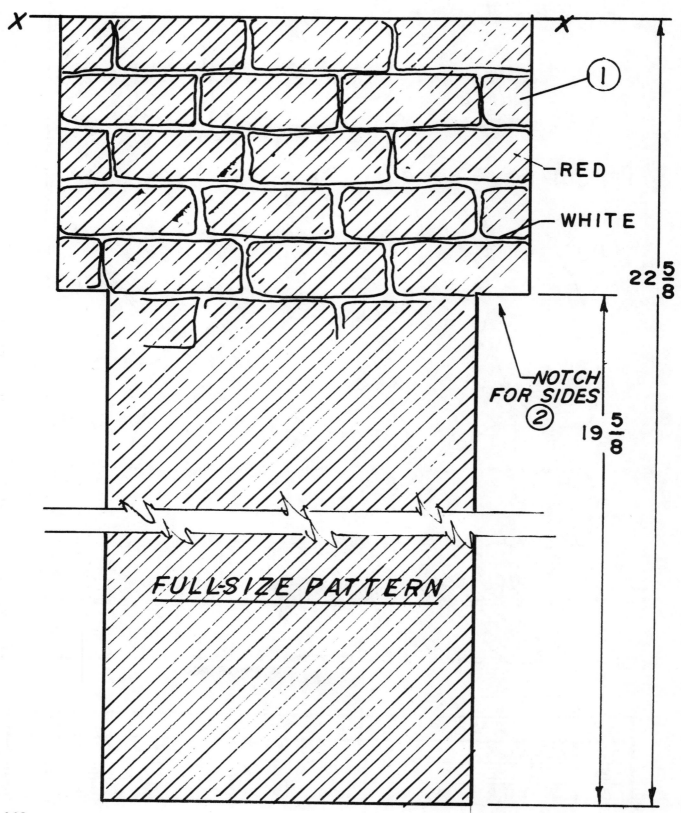

X   X

1

RED

WHITE

$22\frac{5}{8}$

NOTCH
FOR SIDES
2

$19\frac{5}{8}$

FULL-SIZE PATTERN

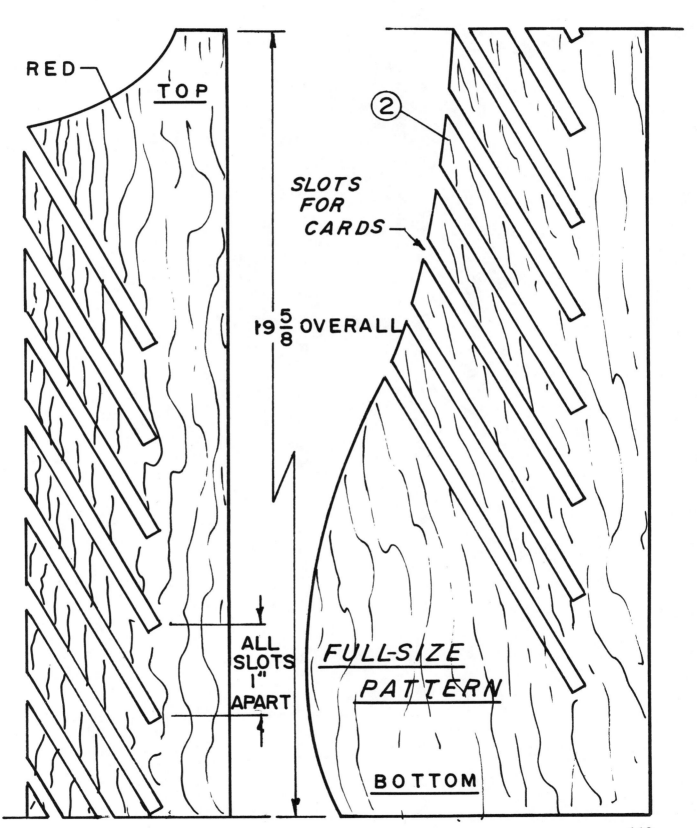

RED

TOP

SLOTS
FOR
CARDS

2

19 $\frac{5}{8}$ OVERALL

ALL
SLOTS
1"
APART

FULL-SIZE
PATTERN

BOTTOM

41♦Snowman Projects

BLACK

RED

YELLOW

BLACK

3/4" THICK

PLAID

YELLOW

RED

WHITE

1/2" THICK

YELLOW

3 1/2" DIA.

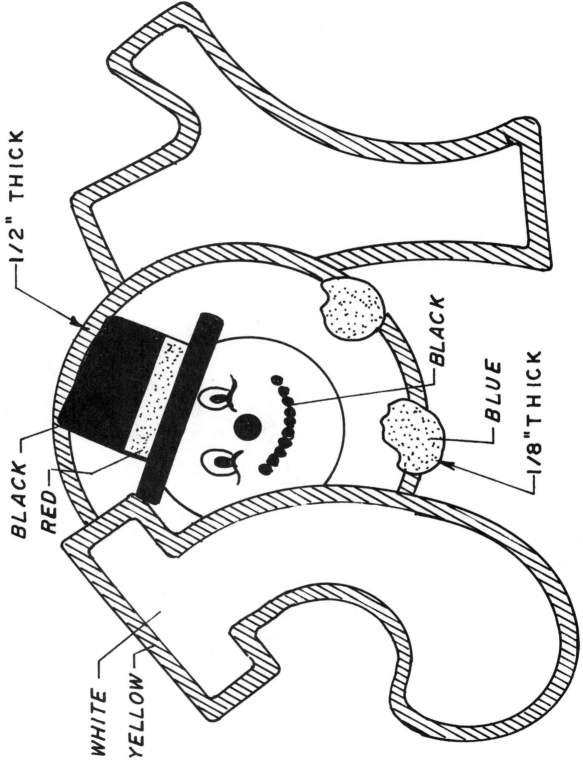

1/2" THICK

BLACK

BLUE

1/8" THICK

BLACK

RED

WHITE

YELLOW

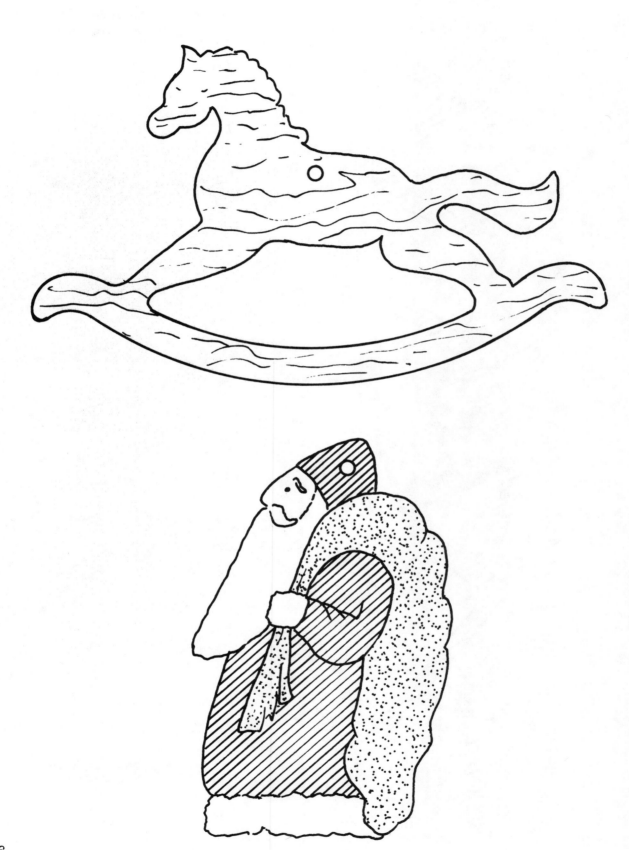

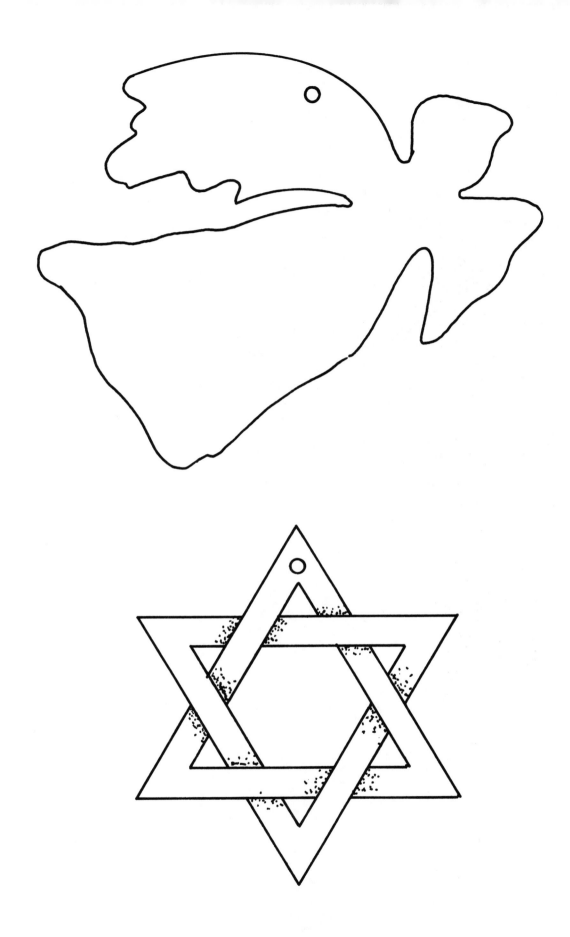

PAINT WITH
BRIGHT COLORS

1/8" DIA. HOLE

43 ◆ Toy Sled

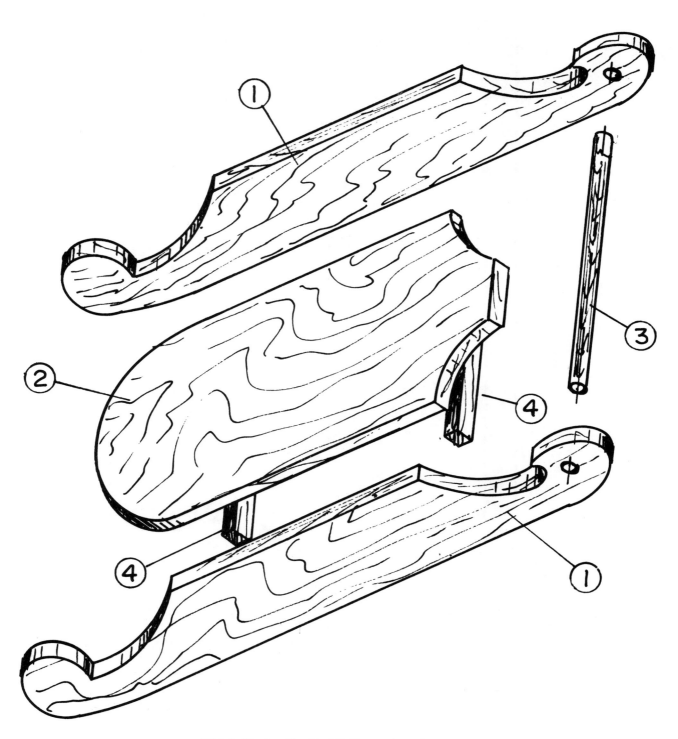

EXPLODED VIEW

TOP VIEW

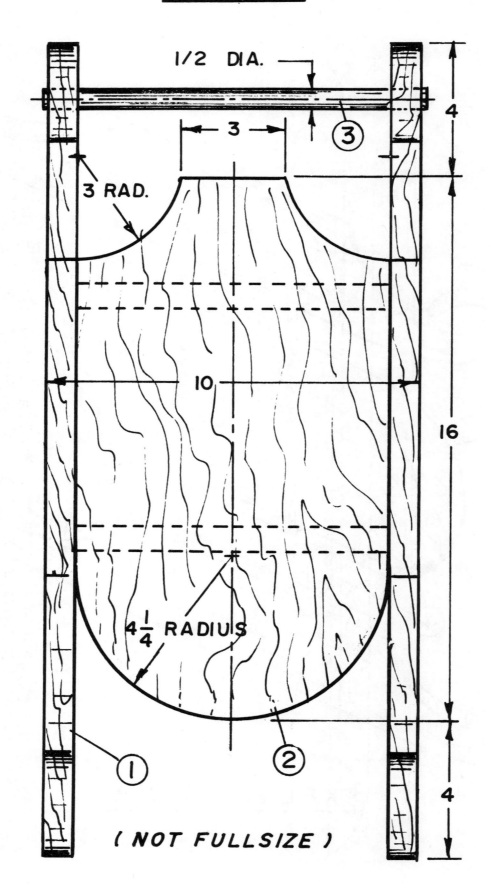

1/2 DIA.

3

③

4

3 RAD.

16

10

4 ¼ RADIUS

① ②

4

(NOT FULLSIZE)

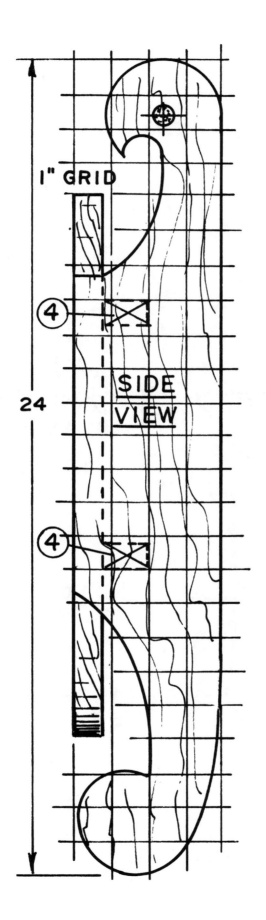

1" GRID

24

SIDE
VIEW

④

④

NO.	NAME	SIZE	REQ'D
1	RUNNER	3/4 X 4 - 24 LONG	2
2	TOP	3/4 X 8 1/2 - 16 LG.	1
3	HANDLE	1/2 DIA. - 10 1/8 LG.	1
4	BRACE	3/4 X 1 1/4 - 8 1/2	2

44◆Hanging Santa

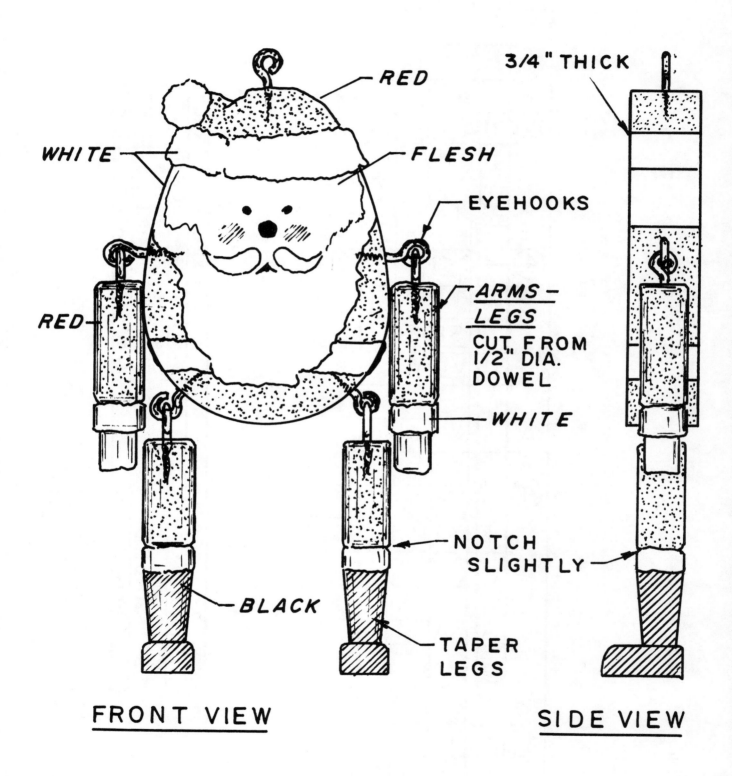

RED

WHITE

FLESH

EYEHOOKS

RED

*ARMS -
LEGS*
CUT FROM
1/2" DIA.
DOWEL

WHITE

BLACK

NOTCH
SLIGHTLY

TAPER
LEGS

FRONT VIEW

3/4" THICK

SIDE VIEW

45 ◆ Skiing Santa

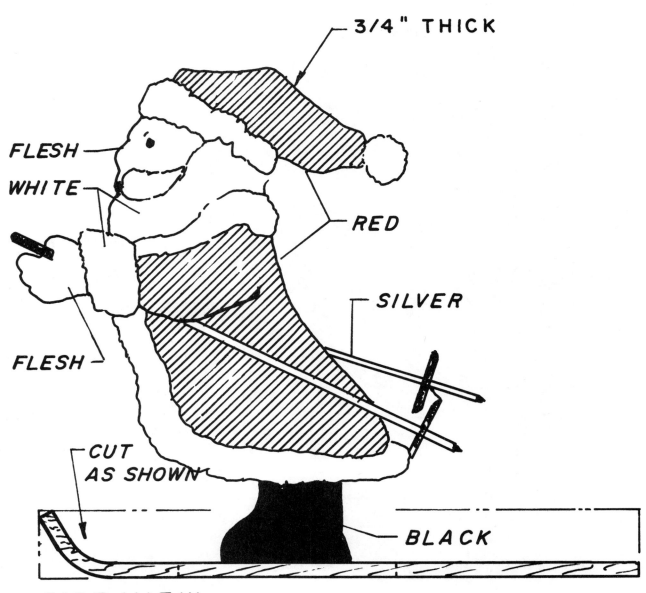

3/4" THICK

FLESH

WHITE

RED

SILVER

FLESH

CUT AS SHOWN

BLACK

SIDE VIEW
CUT TIPS AS SHOWN

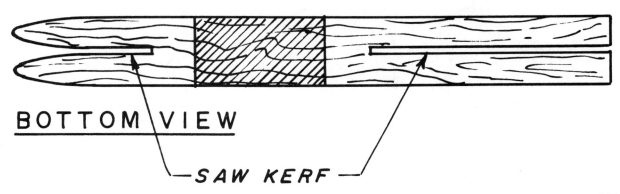

BOTTOM VIEW

SAW KERF

46♦Rocking Santa on a Stand

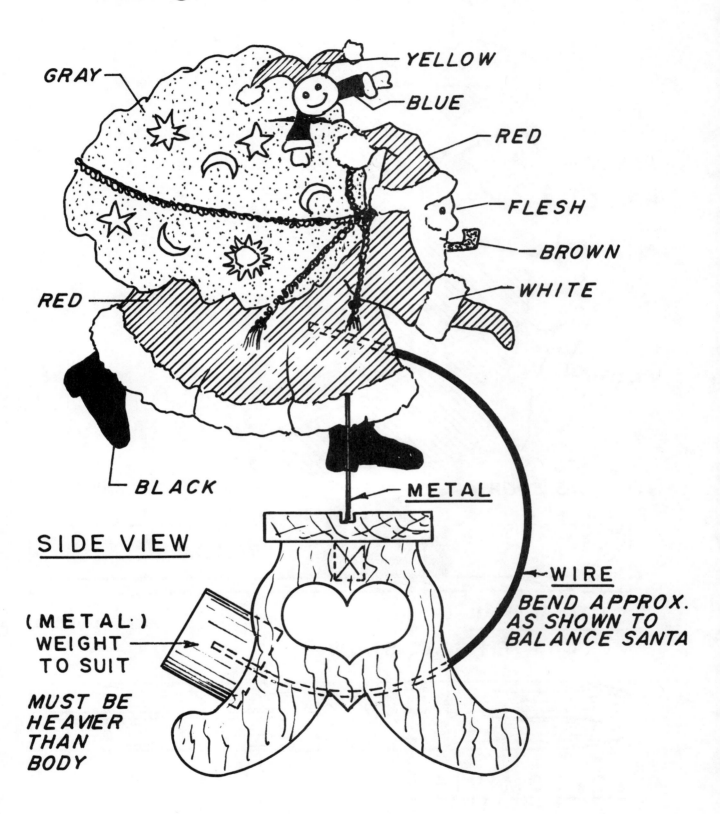

GRAY

YELLOW

BLUE

RED

FLESH

BROWN

WHITE

RED

BLACK

METAL

SIDE VIEW

WIRE

BEND APPROX.
AS SHOWN TO
BALANCE SANTA

(METAL)
WEIGHT
TO SUIT

MUST BE
HEAVIER
THAN
BODY

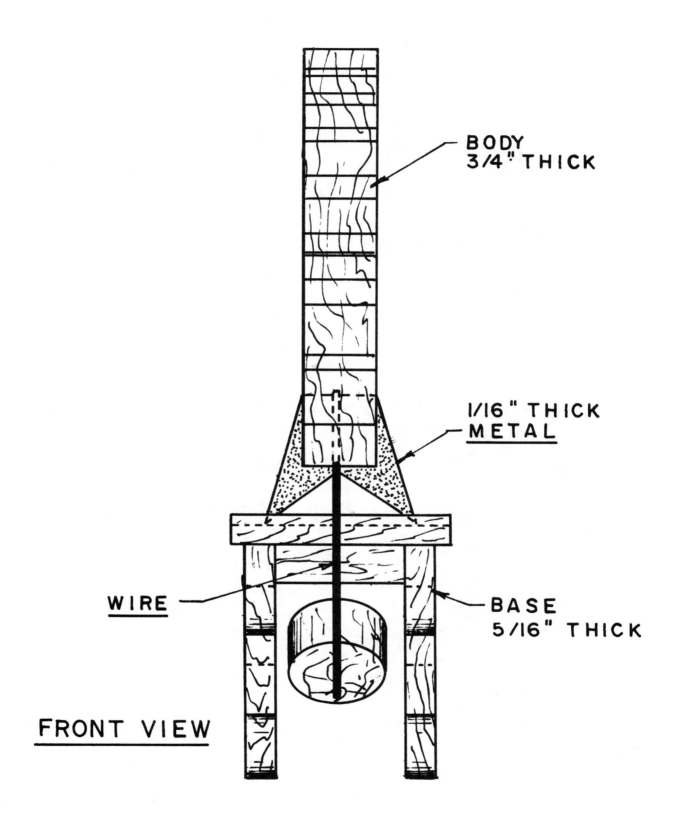

BODY
3/4" THICK

1/16" THICK
METAL

WIRE

BASE
5/16" THICK

FRONT VIEW

47◆Santa Sleigh

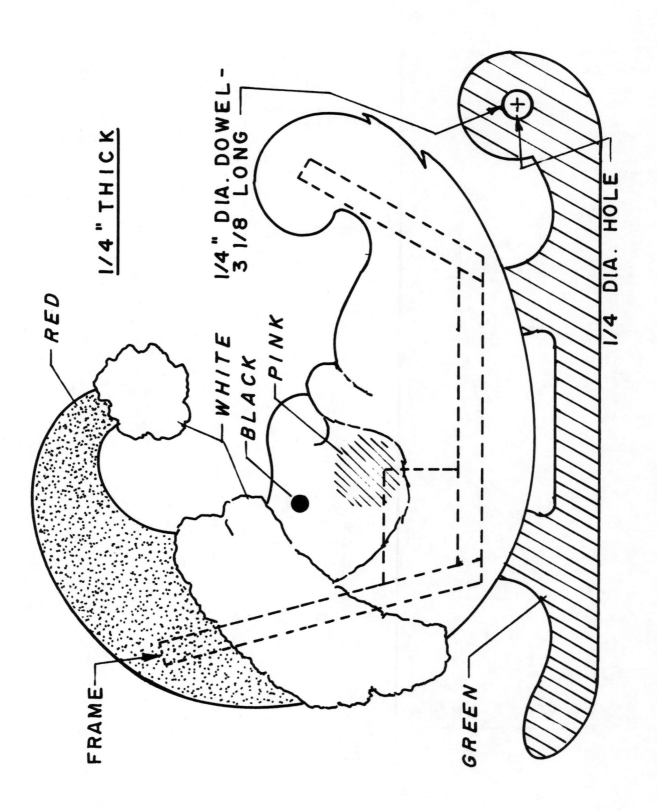

1/4" THICK

1/4" DIA. DOWEL - 3 1/8 LONG

1/4 DIA. HOLE

RED

WHITE

BLACK

PINK

FRAME

GREEN

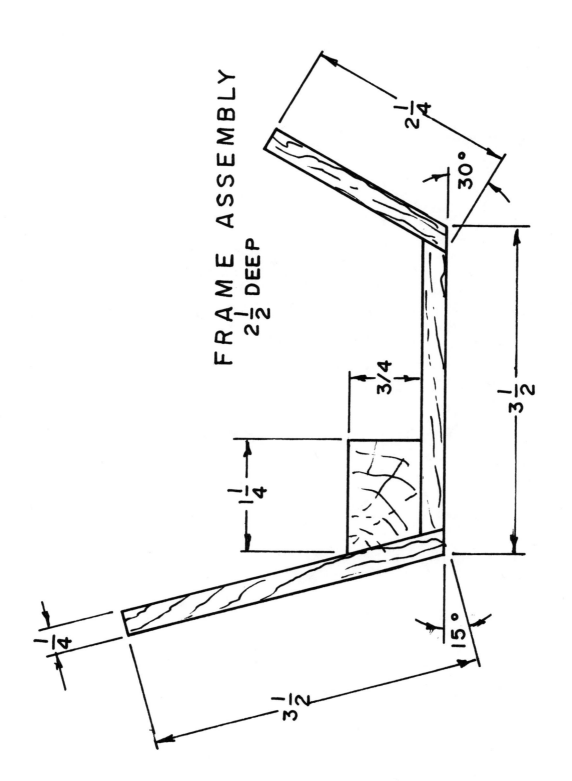

FRAME ASSEMBLY
2½ DEEP

SIDE VIEW

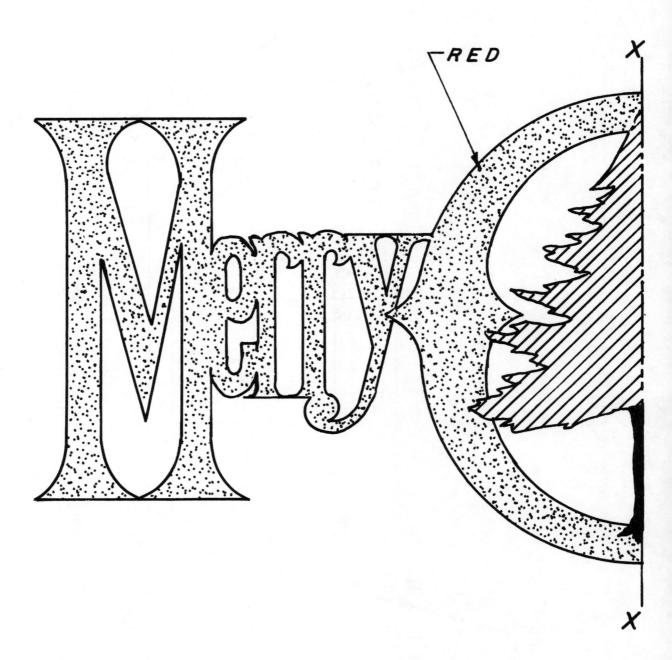

FRONT VIEW

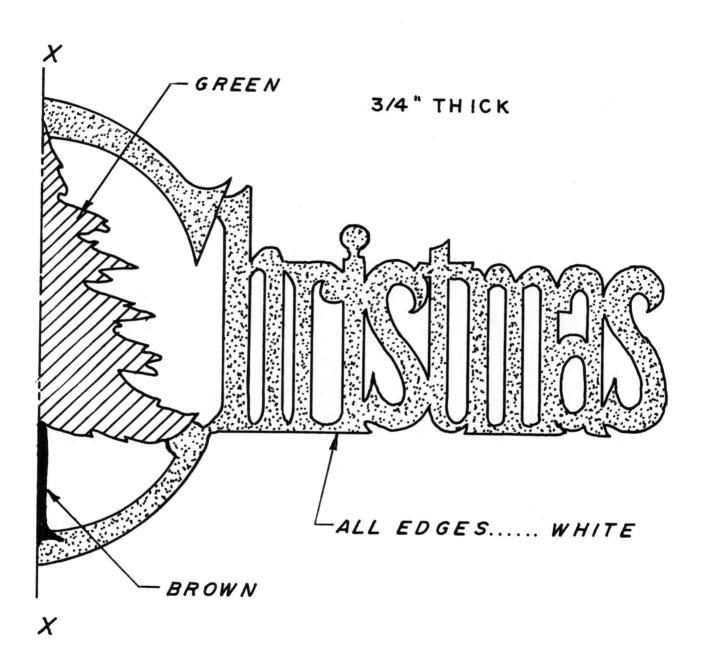

X

GREEN

3/4" THICK

BROWN

ALL EDGES...... WHITE

X

PAINT TO SUIT

X

X

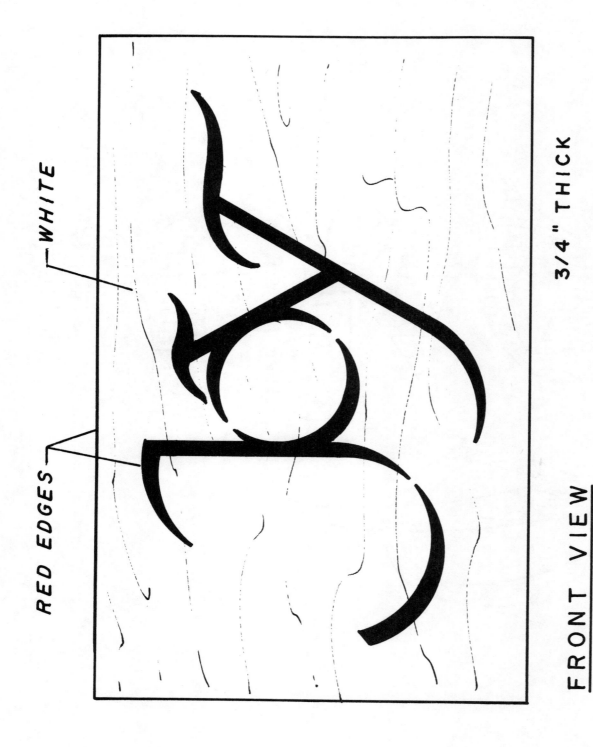

WHITE

RED EDGES

3/4" THICK

FRONT VIEW

134

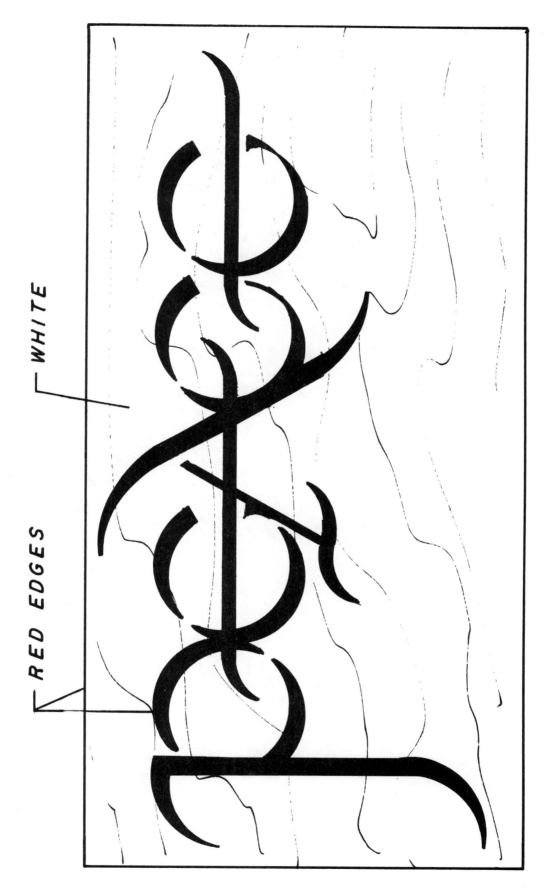

WHITE

RED EDGES

3/4" THICK

FRONT VIEW

135

49 ◆ Candle Menorah

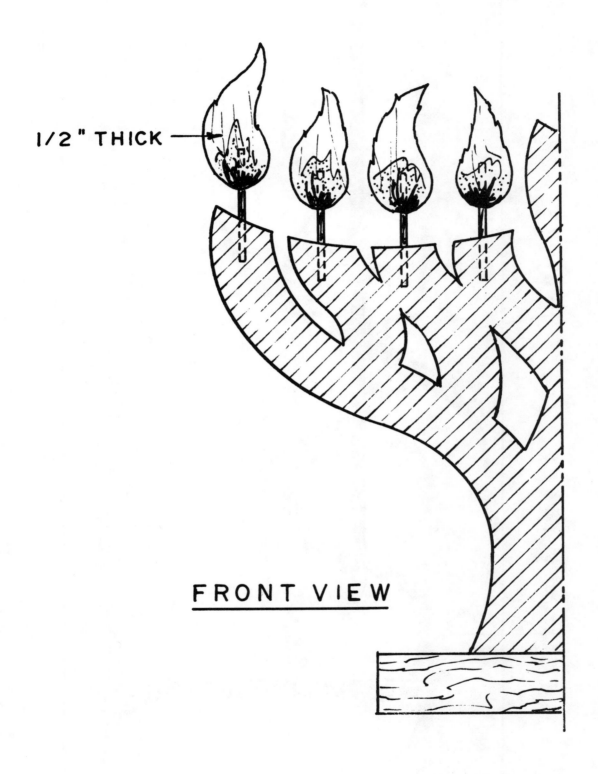

1/2" THICK

FRONT VIEW

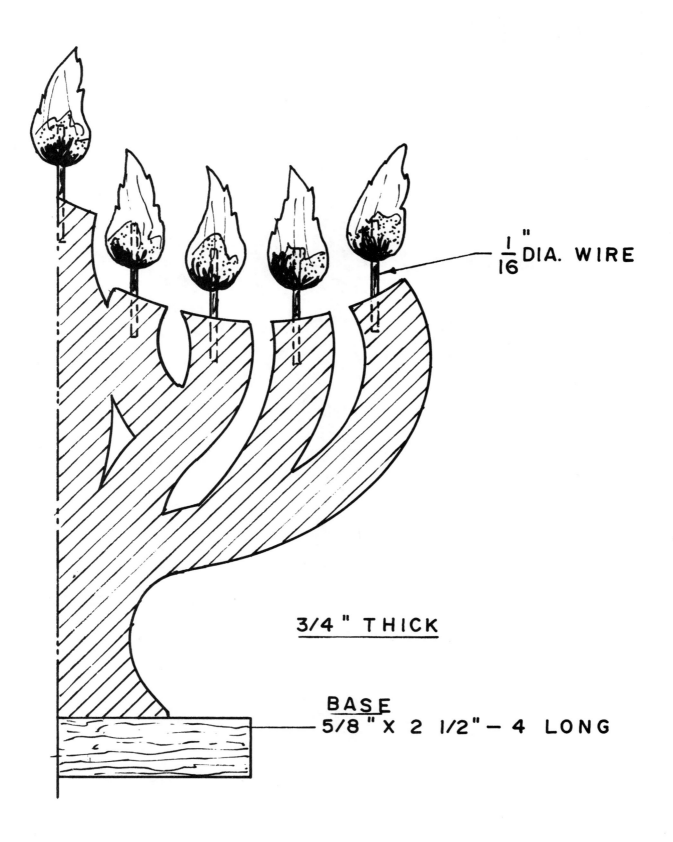

$\frac{1}{16}$" DIA. WIRE

3/4 " THICK

BASE
5/8 " X 2 1/2" — 4 LONG

137

50 ◆ Candy Cane Santa

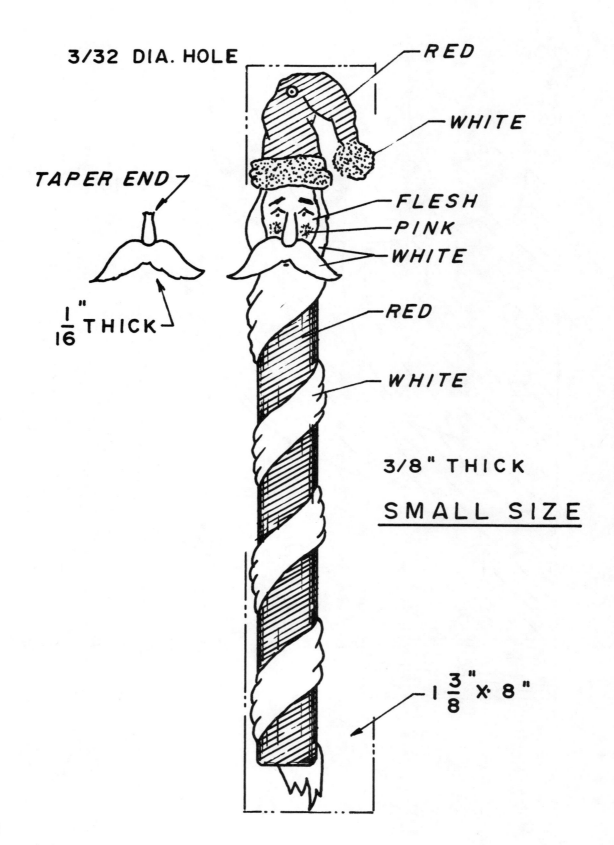

3/32 DIA. HOLE

RED

WHITE

TAPER END

FLESH

PINK

WHITE

RED

WHITE

$\frac{1}{16}$" THICK

3/8" THICK

SMALL SIZE

$1\frac{3}{8}$" x 8"

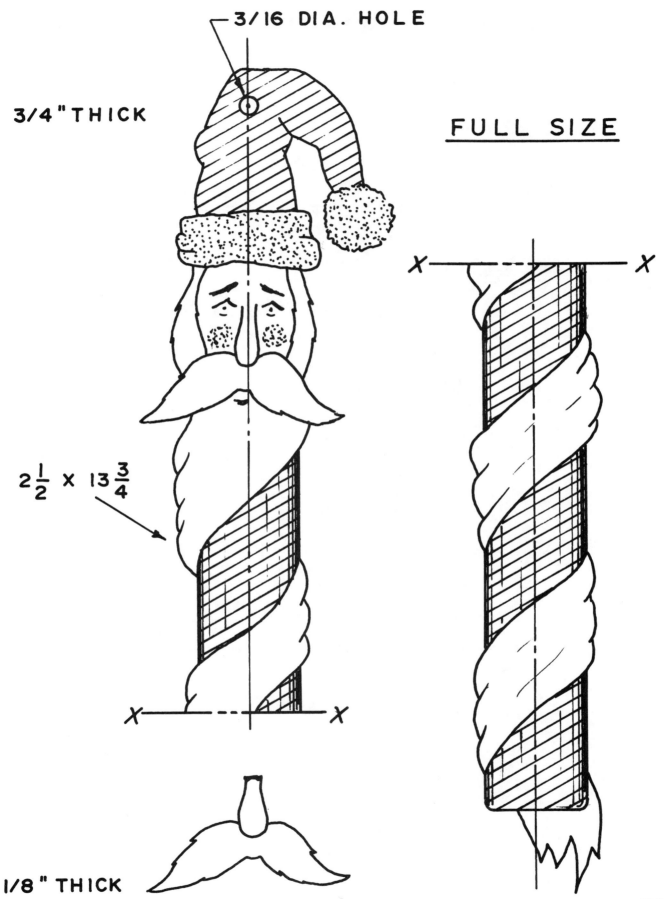

—3/16 DIA. HOLE

3/4" THICK

FULL SIZE

$2\frac{1}{2} \times 13\frac{3}{4}$

1/8" THICK

X———X

X———X

51◆Toy Train with Four Cars

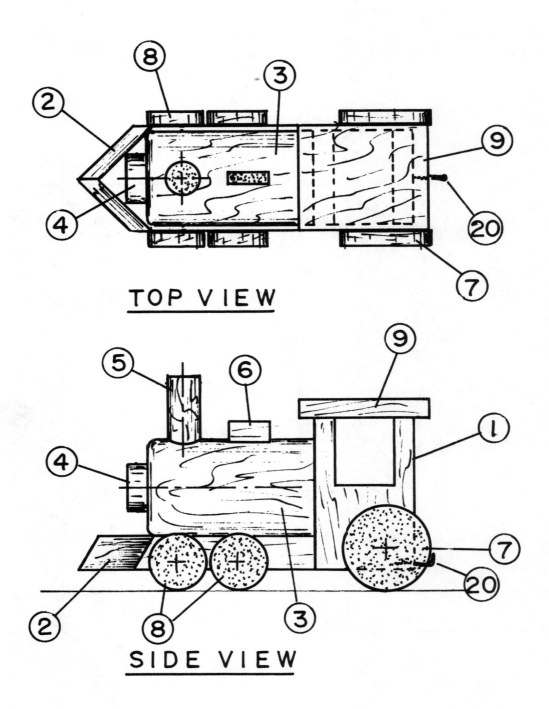

TOP VIEW

SIDE VIEW

FULL SIZE

PAINT WITH BRIGHT COLORS

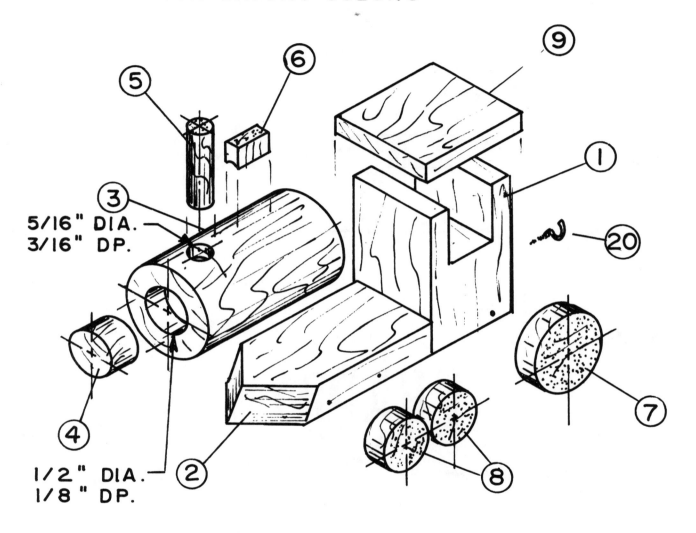

5/16" DIA.
3/16" DP.

1/2" DIA.
1/8" DP.

EXPLODED VIEW

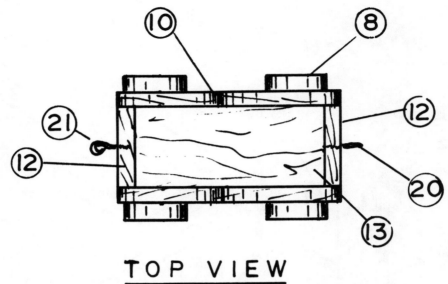

TOP VIEW

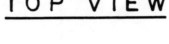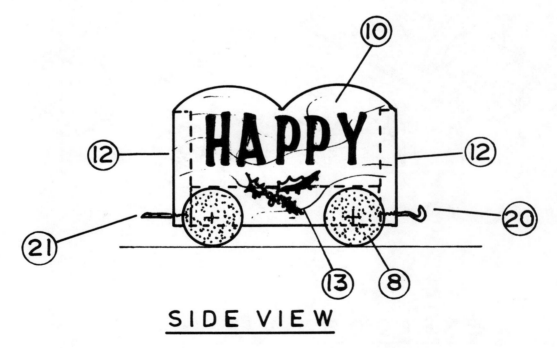

SIDE VIEW

142

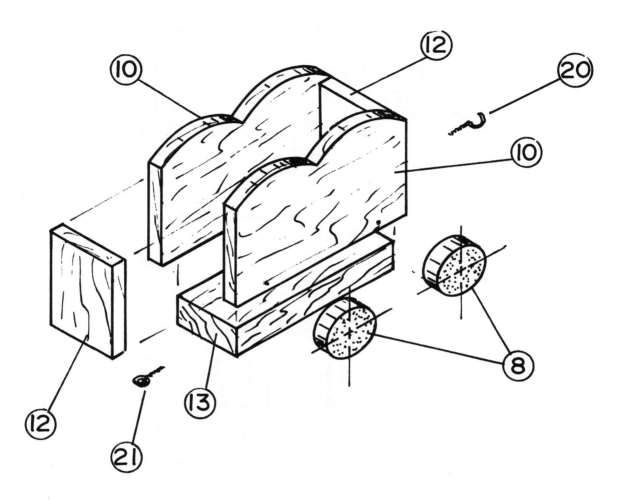

EXPLODED VIEW

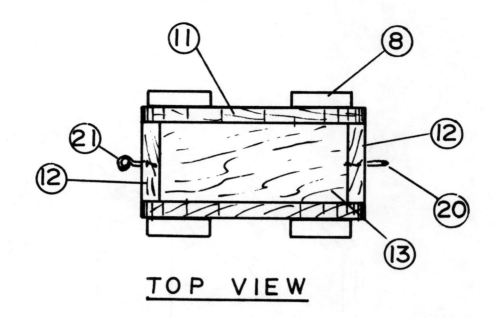

TOP VIEW

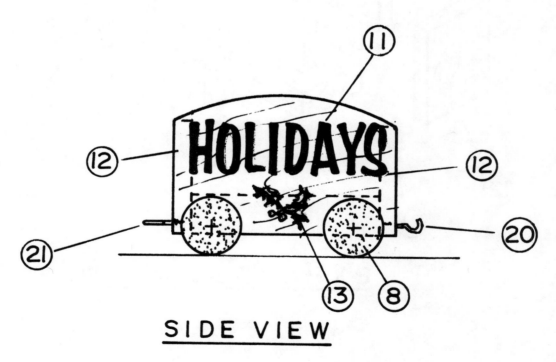

SIDE VIEW

144

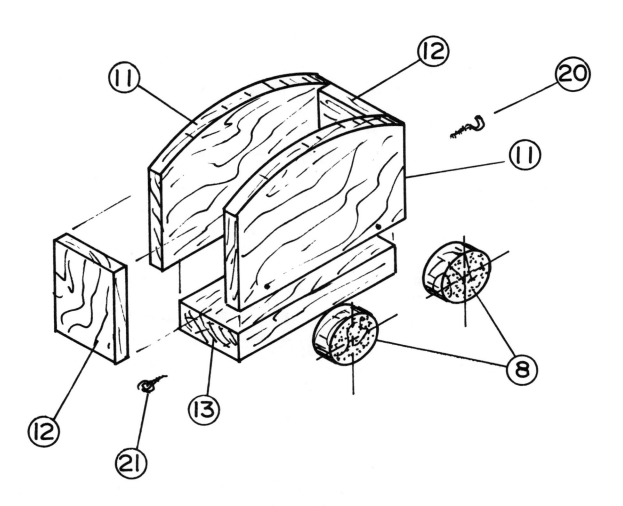

EXPLODED VIEW

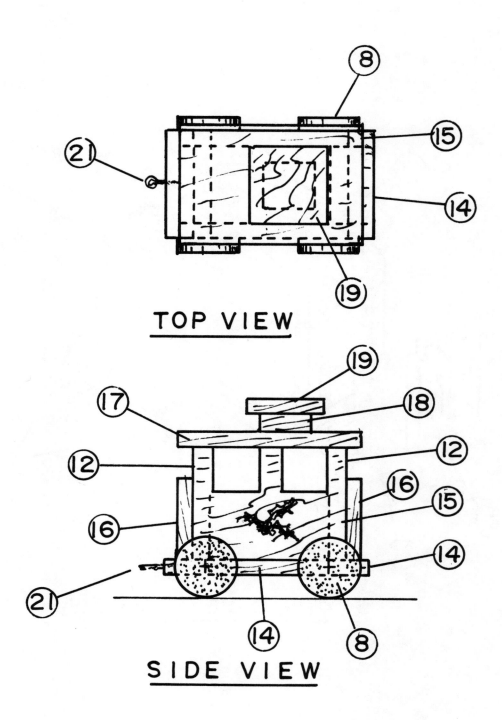

TOP VIEW

SIDE VIEW

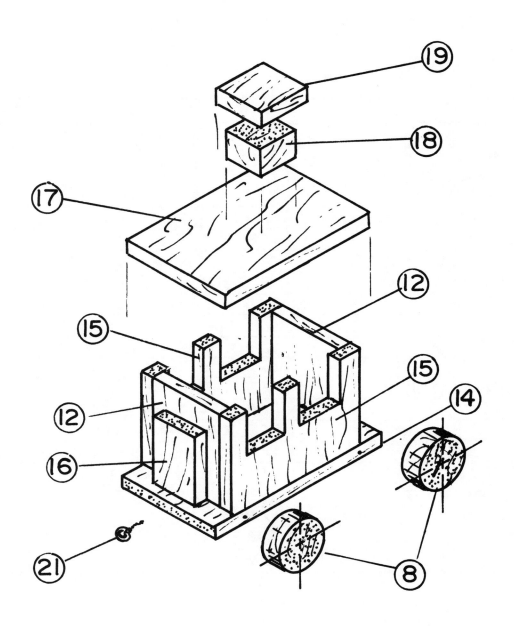

EXPLODED VIEW

NO.	NAME	SIZE	REQ'D.
1	CAB	1 X 1 - 1 5/8 LONG	1
2	BASE	3/8 X 1 - 1 7/8 LG.	1
3	BOILER	1" DIA. X 1 3/4 LG.	1
4	LIGHT	1/2 DIA. X 1/4 LG.	1
5	STACK	5/16 DIA. X 15/16 LG.	1
6	BOX	1/8 X 1/4 - 3/8 LG.	1
7	WHEEL LARGE	7/8 DIA. - 1/8 TK.	2
8	WHEEL SMALL	5/8 DIA. - 1/8 TK.	16
9	ROOF	1/8 X 1 1/8 - 1 3/8 LG.	1
10	SIDE	1/8 X 1 1/2 - 2 1/4 LG.	2
11	SIDE	1/8 X 1 1/2 - 2 1/4 LG.	2
12	END	1/8 X 1 1/4 - 7/8 LG.	6
13	BOTTOM	1/8 X 7/8 - 2 LONG	2
14	BASE	1/8 X 1 1/8 - 2 1/8 LG.	1
15	SIDE	1/8 X 1 1/4 - 1 1/4 LG.	2
16	PLATE	1/8 X 5/8 - 7/8 LONG	2
17	ROOF	1/8 X 1 3/16 - 1 1/2	1
18	LOOKOUT	1/2 X 1/2 - 1/4 LG.	1
19	ROOF	1/8 X 3/4 - 3/4 LONG	1
20	HOOK	SMALL	3
21	EYE	SMALL	3

HAPPY

HOLIDAYS

SPECIAL OCCASION

52♦Happy Birthday Clown

3/4" THICK

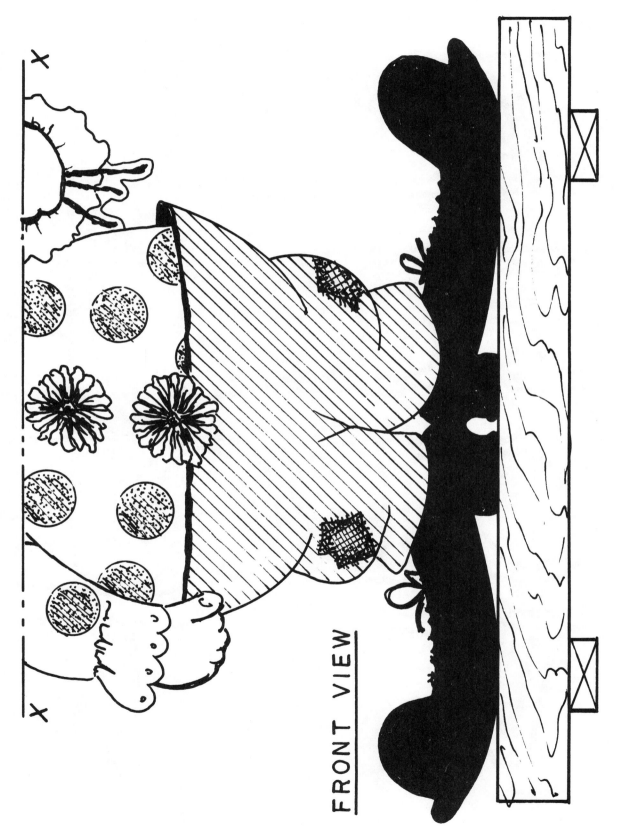

FRONT VIEW

ALPHABETS

A B C

H I J K

O P Q R

V W

D E F G

L M N

S T U

X Y Z

A B C D
J K L M
R S T U
Y Z - ? !

EFGHI

NOPQ

VWX

(-)

ABCDE
LMNO
UVWX
123456

FGHIJK

PQRST

YZ ¢ %

7890 $

Metric Conversion

Inches to Millimetres and Centimetres

MM—millimetres　　　*CM—centimetres*

Inches	MM	CM	Inches	CM	Inches	CM
⅛	3	0.3	9	22.9	30	76.2
¼	6	0.6	10	25.4	31	78.7
⅜	10	1.0	11	27.9	32	81.3
½	13	1.3	12	30.5	33	83.8
⅝	16	1.6	13	33.0	34	86.4
¾	19	1.9	14	35.6	35	88.9
⅞	22	2.2	15	38.1	36	91.4
1	25	2.5	16	40.6	37	94.0
1¼	32	3.2	17	43.2	38	96.5
1½	38	3.8	18	45.7	39	99.1
1¾	44	4.4	19	48.3	40	101.6
2	51	5.1	20	50.8	41	104.1
2½	64	6.4	21	53.3	42	106.7
3	76	7.6	22	55.9	43	109.2
3½	89	8.9	23	58.4	44	111.8
4	102	10.2	24	61.0	45	114.3
4½	114	11.4	25	63.5	46	116.8
5	127	12.7	26	66.0	47	119.4
6	152	15.2	27	68.6	48	121.9
7	178	17.8	28	71.1	49	124.5
8	203	20.3	29	73.7	50	127.0

Index

Other Woodworking Books by John A. Nelson

52 Weekend Woodworking Projects Every one of these woodworking projects can be cut out and assembled over a weekend. From folk-art to heart-shaped projects, from toys and puzzles to clocks and household items—they're all quick and easy to do and require few tools. Almost all of these rewarding projects require only basic woodworking tools, so even beginners can make them easily. Accurate and numbered shop drawings, exploded diagrams, and clear, easy-to-read instructions take you step by step through each project, from selecting materials to putting on finishes. 160 pages.

52 Country Projects for the Weekend Woodworker You can make any of these 52 appealing woodworking projects—each an exact copy of a one-of-a-kind country classic—with basic tools and methods and a minimum of space. Make a sea-horse weather vane, a horse pull toy for a little girl or boy, a Queen Anne mirror as a gift, and many more classic projects. Directions are clear and simple, with detailed exploded construction drawings to illustrate exactly how each piece is made and assembled. You'll learn which materials to select for each project, the right joinery methods, the tools you'll need, finishing hints, and a whole host of other practical workshop techniques. 160 pages.

52 Decorative Weekend Woodworking Projects Add some variety to your weekend woodworking with these 52 unique, quick, and easy projects! From toys and games to folk-art objects, and from practical household items to country favorites, you'll find everything you could possibly ask for in this one guide! Each project comes with full-size patterns, two- and three-view drawings of front and side and top, and exploded diagrams and section views of moulding details and techniques for joining parts. Every part is numbered, so you can see exactly where each one goes. Other time-savers: a bill of materials listed in order of use, with shortcuts for making duplicate pieces and transferring patterns to wood, as well as for enlarging or reducing any project to suit your needs. 160 pages.

52 Toys & Puzzles for the Weekend Woodworker This is a fun-filled book of 52 toys—toys for children of all ages 6 to 60. There are toys of today, puzzles and tricks, toys of yesterday, and even folk-art toys. Included are a train, tool box, log cabin, circus truck with animals, lots of great pull toys, and even a rocking horse and walking seesaw. The projects range from very simple-to-make toys to somewhat more difficult-to-make toys, but all are designed for the typical weekend home crafter. 8 pages in color. 168 pages.